How to be
Asked Again

How to be Asked Again

How to be the Perfect Shooting Guest

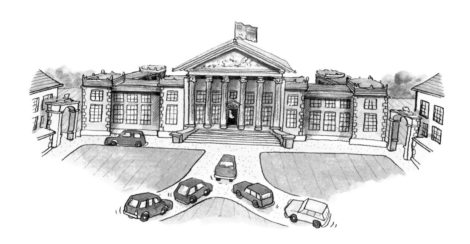

Rosie Nickerson
Illustrations by
Oliver Preston

Quiller

Text copyright © 2009 Rosie Nickerson
Illustrations copyright © 2009 Oliver Preston

First published in the UK in 2009
by Quiller, an imprint of Quiller Publishing Ltd
Reprinted 2009

British Library Cataloguing-in-Publication Data
    A catalogue record for this book
    is available from the British Library

ISBN 978 1 84689 057 4

The right of Rosie Nickerson to be identified as the author of this work has been
asserted in accordance with the Copyright, Design and Patent Act 1988

The information in this book is true and complete to the best of our knowledge.
All recommendations are made without any guarantee on the part of the Publisher,
who also disclaims any liability incurred in connection with the use of this data or
specific details.

Printed in China

Quiller

An imprint of Quiller Publishing Ltd
Wykey House, Wykey, Shrewsbury, SY4 1JA
Tel: 01939 261616 Fax: 01939 261606
E-mail: info@quillerbooks.com
Website: www.countrybooksdirect.com

Dedication

I would like to dedicate this book to my father,
who introduced me to the world of shooting and
conservation.

Acknowledgements

The title *How to be Asked Again* was inspired by an amusing book which was given to me as a young girl. Published in 1979 by Debretts, *I'll Never Be Asked Again* was about a young Canadian girl who goes grouse shooting for the first time with her English fiancé and gets everything wrong…

I'd been steeped in the world of shooting from a very young age. My father, the late Sir Joseph Nickerson, often went shooting six days out of seven. He encouraged my sisters and me to accompany him from about the age of five. My father taught us far more than just how to shoot. He introduced us gradually to all aspects of shooting, including field craft, marking your birds, dog-handling, conservation and good manners on the field. I am extremely grateful to him for providing me with such a complete and well-rounded shooting education.

The seeds of the idea for writing the book were sown when I met a successful entrepreneur, James Lancaster, at a shoot in Wales in 2006. 'I shudder to think of all the mistakes I used to make', he remarked at lunch, recalling how ignorant he had been on his first day's driven shooting some twenty years earlier. I started thinking about what James had told me: not everyone who takes up shooting has the advantage of a long 'country apprenticeship'. This was the catalyst for me writing the book.

When I started casting about for a publisher I was lucky enough that Richard Purdey recommended Andrew Johnston at Quiller Publishing. Fortunately he liked the idea and took the book on.

My task would have been impossible without the help of the many people whose voices you will hear within the book's pages. They come from a broad range of shooting spheres: beaters, flankers, keepers, pickers-up, loaders, instructors, shoot organisers, shoot owners, spectators and gun-dealers, as well as some of the country's keenest and best known shots. The majority of the advice, stories, and 'dos and don'ts' came from them. They have transformed the book into what I hope will be an amusing and entertaining read. There will undoubtedly be some omissions, certain people whose words I should have included, but even so the tally amounts to more than seventy separate interviews. Thank you to all of you for your contributions.

To Oliver Preston, the cartoonist and illustrator, I would like to say how delighted I am to have had the chance to work with him. His twin talents for observing the minutiae of shooting life and his artistic ability are a rare combination.

A big thank you, too, to those who were always on the end of the phone or an e-mail when I needed advice, telephone numbers and information. I can't mention everyone by name, but Jonathan Kennedy, Nick Fane, David Hicks, Jonathan Young and Mike Barnes were all incredibly helpful.

I would also like to say a huge thank you to my friends who agreed to help out with the first drafts, by reading some of the chapters prior to me sending them off. In particular financial journalist Philippa Aylmer deserves special mention.

Thanks also to John Beaton who waited and waited for the book to be finished and to Kirsty Ennever, whose attention to detail and friendly professionalism was characteristic of all the team at Quiller.

To my long-suffering husband and fellow shot, Piers: thank you for all your help and encouragement along the way. (I promised him I wouldn't ever write another book but I think he knows I was lying…)

Thank you, too, to my three children – James, Alicia and Louis – who all took a great interest in 'Mummy's book' and whose homework occasionally had to take a back seat. I could not have juggled looking after them had it not been for the support of my mother, Erna Nickerson, and my au pair, Pinar Dal.

Rosie Nickerson
London

Contents

Introduction

'Your job as a guest is to make it a great party. It's a serious duty. You must be really enthusiastic about the shooting and add some humour and wit to the day.'
Jonathan Young

Game shooting for anyone new to the sport is fraught with potential pitfalls. Aside from the obvious one of safety, there are so many subtle but essential courtesies on the shooting-field which it is vital to know, but which cannot be taught at a shooting school. You must be fully aware of them though to be properly accepted – and most importantly, invited again. These largely unwritten rules can be hard to learn for the novice Gun, especially if no one tells him what they are: no one will want to embarrass the newcomer by explaining how things work on the day. That's the irony, the novice only works out that he must have done something wrong when the invitations dry up. Unless, of course, he's just bought a huge grouse moor, in which case people may well turn a blind eye!

Knowing how to behave out shooting is absolutely crucial if you ever hope to be asked again. Few other sports make you quite so dependent on return invitations in order to be able to practise them, so you can see why doing the right thing on the field is so vital.

Unless you own your own shoot, or belong to a good syndicate, then your only hope of shooting regularly and often is to buy a day of your own, invite all your chums and then hope to be invited back as a guest. If you are lucky enough to know people with plenty of shooting though, you may be invited again and again purely because you are good company and know the form. There are some fortunate people like this, who travel all over the country from 12 August to 1 February, flitting from shoot to shoot with the ease and grace of a butterfly. They arrive on time, with the right kit, shoot straight, greet the beaters, charm the keeper, dispense encouragement to novice shots and keep everyone entertained. They are always appreciative to their host, never moaning if they aren't in the thick of it, shoot consistently and well, never being too greedy, and mark and pick their own birds as well as helping others pick theirs. These perfect guests do not get plastered at lunchtime either and they always remember to tip the keeper generously at the end of the day.

'The perfect guest is someone who is fun, someone who brings something to the party; this is more important than if they are a good shot', says Sir Edward Dashwood, top shot and shoot host.

As a shooting guest, if you are fraught with nerves and terrified of cocking up, you do not have a hope of being charming or entertaining: you will be so anxious not to put a foot wrong that you will probably be about as much fun as yesterday's newspaper. Alternatively, if you just don't care enough about the courtesies to want to get them right, then your diary is destined to be a snowscape come the shooting season.

For any shooting host, it is immensely relaxing to know that he has at least one Gun in the team who can be trusted one hundred per cent to be the perfect guest: someone on whom he can rely at all times. He would probably gladly invite that person year after year, regardless of what shooting was offered in return. The only Guns I've ever come across who fit into this category have invariably been shooting since they were very young and so have had a long apprenticeship: following the keepers, going beating, and eventually earning the right to stalk the hedgerows with a single barrel 4.10. While this might have been a slow process, the Gun will have gradually absorbed all that goes into a shooting day and had the chance to learn about every aspect of field-craft, including marking birds and picking up. If proper respect for safety and shooting etiquette is drilled into you from the cradle it becomes second nature.

Few may have had the benefit of an upbringing like this, but anyone can learn the ropes as an adult. The popularity of driven game shooting has soared. Over one million of us are involved in the sport in this country and, according to Countryside Alliance figures, it contributes around £1.6 billion to the rural economy. Until the 2008 credit crunch, shooting was *the* sport of choice for corporate entertaining. Some of the biggest names in the corporate world took shoot days and in a big way. Whilst this was fabulous for the future of the sport, it nevertheless caused a real surge in people coming on to the shooting field who were new to it. At times this made for some very poor sportsmanship on the field.

One of the aims of this book is to enable the novice Gun to bypass twenty or more long years of apprenticeship, so that he can immediately become the sort of guest whom shooting hosts want to invite time and time again. *How to be Asked Again* is compiled from a vast array of titbits gleaned from conversations with over seventy people, some are named, others prefer to stay anonymous. Each of them has told me what, in their eyes, makes the perfect guest out shooting. Their advice, personal experiences and often hilarious anecdotes will hopefully provide all the information any aspiring Gun will ever need to become The Perfect Guest.

1
The Shooting Invitation

'Never send out your shooting invitations before Ascot week'
Old shooting maxim

You have just received a letter inviting you to shoot!

'How marvellous! What an honour! That will be fun', you think. But before you do anything else, and certainly before you forget all about it thinking, 'Oh, it's not for ages', it is vital to respond immediately.

Piffa Schroder, shot, author and long-time contributor to *Shooting Gazette* says:

'The really attentive guest will answer any shooting invitation by return of post – if it's done any later, it always looks as if you're waiting to see whether a more attractive invitation from somewhere else turns up…'

If you already know you can't make the date, reply as soon as you can. In the past, the only way to issue a shooting invitation was by handwritten letter. Should you receive one like this, then it is still good form to respond in the same way. Typed shooting invitations are not of course so personal to receive, but obviously very busy people often have teams of secretaries to deal with such things. To my mind even a scrawled note with just a date, time and place on it is preferable. However, these days many people like the speed and efficiency of e-mail, which is becoming a more and more acceptable way to send out your shooting invitations. Sometimes you will just receive a telephone call, although this does tend to put you on the spot.

Regardless of how you are invited, you must respond quickly. If you have to refuse, your host can then invite someone else immediately and with any luck the substitute will never realise that he is second choice.

To accept or not to accept?

Assuming you plan to accept, first make absolutely sure that you are free. Shooting invitations can be issued at least six or even twelve months in advance and it is vital to check your diary in minute detail, so that in your eagerness to reply, you don't accidentally double-book yourself. Experienced shots all say that it is far better to refuse and live to regret it, than to accept and have to cancel later. That is one of the fastest ways to ensure that you won't be asked again, and you may even jeopardise a friendship.

Be warned that by accepting an invitation to shoot, you may well be starting an eternal game of shoot 'ping-pong'. However tempting it might be to shoot at a particular place, if you don't like the host enough to want to invite him back to anything, then politely refuse the invitation. It really is 'a shot for a shot' and it is poor form to accept an invitation in the full knowledge that you will never reciprocate. The shooting world is a village and you don't want to be known as 'a bit of a taker'.

Once you have accepted – don't duck out!

It goes without saying that once you have accepted, only death – your own or a close family member's – should stop you attending on the day. Having said that, my father's view, which he states in his book *A Shooting Man's Creed*, was that a streaming cold could be an acceptable reason for a no-show:

> 'Nobody will thank you for turning up at a shoot with a highly infectious cold and this is especially true when some of the guests are elderly, because what may be only seven days of snuffles for a young man may be six weeks of bronchitis for an older person.'

Many people will have heard of the practical joke a group of friends played on a very well-known shot who was apparently gaining a bit of a reputation for accepting an invitation and then declining it if a better one came up. He was caught out when he turned up on the preferred day to find that all the other Guns, whose shoots he had declined one by one for this big day, were shooting there too, and the whole thing had been planned to teach him a lesson! The moral of this story is that it is NEVER worth wriggling out of a shoot because you later receive what you take to be a 'better' invitation.

Even worse than this is to accept an invitation and then just not turn up. I heard a story recently about this happening. The host had even discussed all the plans for the shoot with the guest in question on the phone the week before, but on the day he just never appeared. Apparently he has never apologised or offered any explanation and sadly the two have not spoken since.

Getting it wrong

Someone told me another story about a Gun who goes shooting, has a wonderful day, is relaxing at home afterwards and is surprised when a friend rings up to find out why the hell he never turned up at his shoot. 'But I was shooting at Fred's today,' the Gun replied. The friend was very peeved and reiterated that he'd definitely been expected at *his* shoot that day. So the Gun rings up the host where he'd just been.

'Fred, were you expecting me today or not?' he asked.

'Well, to tell you the truth, no we weren't, but we were a Gun short, so it didn't matter in the least. Why?' asked Fred.

The moral of the story is, always write down the name and place where you are meant to be shooting in your diary the moment you have accepted the invitation. Committing the date to memory is clearly not foolproof.

On accepting

Once you've accepted, check the location of the shoot if you have not been there before. Don't just guess its location, as so many people do to their cost, and beware of 'sat navs' as certain estates share their names with totally unrelated towns! Unless you have the correct postcode, you could, as one of our guests did, end up in Rothwell, Leeds, rather than in Rothwell, Lincolnshire: he has never been allowed to forget his blunder.

If you haven't been invited to arrive the night before, ask yourself whether you can comfortably get there and back in a day. A general rule of thumb is that anywhere further than two hours away from your home will mean you should plan to stay somewhere locally to be sure of getting to the shoot on time.

A shot for a shot

Whoever has invited you in a particular year, or the year before, should be considered as a priority for you to invite back during the following season or at least the one after that. As mentioned earlier, there is a huge *quid pro quo* side to shooting.

When planning your line of Guns, of course you will want to invite your best mates to shoot. However it does help if some of them have their own shoots, or shoot days too, as otherwise you will find your diary rather empty the following season! A good mix of people is probably the best bet. I try to invite some Guns who are shoot owners or who regularly buy shoot days; and some who are friends who may not have access to shooting at all, but whose company I enjoy for its own sake. Inviting friends shooting is a great way to catch up with those who have moved away, or live abroad: a shoot day will bring you all together like no other occasion.

I have never, and will never, invite anyone to shoot whom I do not like, just in order to shoot their fabulous pheasants or grouse.

Geoffrey Palmer, a well-known shot from Norfolk, has the same view, declaring that he is 'not prepared to accept anyone's invitation to shoot whom I am not prepared to invite back'. This is absolutely right, because the moment you accept an invitation, you are indebted to that person. If you have a shoot and never ask them back, it is considered very rude. Of course if you don't have access to shooting yourself, perhaps you could invite your hosts to some other treat, such as the theatre, or a weekend away.

Palmer's own style of issuing invitations is renowned for its eccentricity. First, he gives you a choice of about ten or twelve dates a long way ahead, up to a year sometimes, and then often lists his own available dates when he can accept *your* shooting on the invitation letter! This may seem eminently practical but it also causes some raised eyebrows and general hilarity amongst the shooting fraternity. Whilst this technique won't be found in any guide to shooting etiquette, it is nevertheless expedient and honest, enabling a guest to pick and choose the date which suits him best and also see immediately when Palmer is free.

Some shoot owners operate an alternate year invitation system, which avoids any awkwardness if you have been inviting your friend Sam Shot for years consecutively and then one year you decide to invite someone else for a change. He might take huge offence, because he has come to expect that he will be shooting with you every year. Good friends, who will be good company but to whom you don't necessarily 'owe' any shooting, should really come second to those whom you do 'owe'. There is also the tricky business of people whose invitations you haven't been able to accept; do you then 'owe' them? My advice is that if you want them to ask you again, you must invite them first, as a refused invitation is still an invitation.

Corporate entertaining is entirely different. A client will be invited purely to strengthen business links and a working relationship. Even so, there is no such thing as a free lunch especially in the world of shooting, where even a modest day of 100 birds will set the host back £3,000 to £4,000. The cost of some of the bigger days which attract the corporate market can easily rise to £10,000 or more, excluding any hotel expenses.

The done thing

Many shoot hosts are very successful in their careers. They are highly organised in their business lives and tend to follow the same principles when it comes to shooting. Naturally they want to make sure that the guest of their choice will be able to come. It would seem to make sense, then, to offer guests more than one date, but this is not the usual practice in the shooting world.

Lady Celestria Noel, social expert and a former editor of *Harper's Bazaar* magazine's Jennifer's Diary, says:

'I don't think you should overwhelm your guest with dates, it's rude as they can't get out of it. With weddings and most social occasions, invitations go out six weeks before. With shooting, it is crucial to get the numbers right, you've got to try and plan ahead. There are no definite rules on this, but I think you can say that the grander the shoot and the grander the Gun, the further ahead you ask them for. If you have a less grand shoot and a younger more casual crowd, then a shorter notice period is fine, say two to three months ahead. But you've really got to get in early. Plan ahead, ask yourself which are your best days, who are your ideal guests? Some smaller rough shoots might only ask you the day before!'

One old shooting maxim, before the age of reared birds, was 'never send out your shooting invitations before Ascot week'. This was because the weather in mid-June determined how the partridge chicks would fare. Rain and cold that week always means a poor wild partridge stock.

The B list

Inevitably, people do drop out of shoot days, despite the huge black mark incurred by a 'no show'. On the whole, shoot hosts seem to prefer to ask another Gun rather than shoot with less people. However, an invitation for less than two or three weeks ahead will simply not be viewed in the same light by the recipients. They will know that they are not your first choice and although they may assure you that they don't mind at all, the truth is, they really will. In fact unless you really do need a full line of Guns, for instance for grouse shooting in a year when stocks need to be reduced (when you should feel proud that your shooting prowess is required) hosts should ask themselves if they really do need another Gun.

Of course if it is a syndicate shoot and the 'last-minute' Gun would be paying his way, then those rules don't apply. The moment money changes hands, it is no longer considered an invitation but is purely a business transaction – however exclusive the shoot, or 'lucky' the Gun is to be allowed to participate.

Grouse shooting – a different kettle of fish

Last minute grouse shooting invitations are quite different. The sheer unpredictability of grouse stocks is the reason many moor owners only invite their guests in June for August or September. By June there will be a fair indication of stocks but only in July, when the formal counts are done, does the keeper feel able to predict how many days that season will be available. It is a very imprecise science and sometimes, come September or October, there are more – or less – birds around than the keeper first predicted. So don't ever feel second best if you only get your grouse shooting invitation a month or even a couple of weeks ahead. Some very skilled grouse shots will get only a week's or a few days' notice in a good season, because often extra days are put on if the keeper wants to reduce stock size.

'Sometimes I think you only married me for my father's grouse moor.'

The Duke of Northumberland, grouse moor owner and accomplished shot, says:

'I often get last-minute invitations. I love it, particularly late October grouse invitations. I don't even mind if they ring the day before! And I wouldn't hesitate to invite someone at the last minute if I needed to.'

One Yorkshire grouse moor owner always seems to send his grouse shooting invitations out in April. Then, in about July, he often has to write regretfully informing his guests that the days have been cancelled, brood sizes not being what he had hoped they would be. By this time of course he has clocked up a fair few invitations of his own – by writing to all his shoot-owning friends so early on, they naturally feel compelled to ask him to their shoots!

It's all in the words

If you are the one issuing the invitation, always be factual, give the date, the location, whether you will be having the guest to stay, and whether their partner is welcome too.
For example:

'We would be delighted if you could join us to shoot some pheasants at Wriggley Bottom on Saturday, 12 January. We will meet at the pub in the village at 9.15am and we will be having lunch there at 1pm. Henrietta is very welcome to join us.'

It is always polite to include partners where applicable; equally if the day is for an all-male team (or all-female!) make this clear too to avoid any misunderstandings.

Shooting couples

If you are inviting a couple who both shoot, and you have only one place in the line to offer them, don't feel it is rude to ask them to share a peg. Speaking from experience (as one half of a shooting couple) both will be delighted to be included. Offering a shared peg is far more diplomatic than to ask only one or the other, or worse, to ask the other to come just for lunch! Shooting couples know only too well

that taking up two spaces in the line will be difficult for the shoot host who no doubt has plenty of people to invite. A father and son or mother and daughter will similarly be happy to share a peg. If you are having a day with other youngsters, but you want the parent to come too, just write: 'Do share a gun'. When invited to share in this way, never assume that this means you will both be shooting at the same time from the same peg. Correct form is either to shoot on alternate drives, or have a system of, say, ten shots each and then swap, or something along those lines.

Double-gun days

If it is to be a double-gun day, do mention this in the invitation, e.g.: 'It will be a double-gun day and we will provide a loader unless you would like to bring your own.' In this case, make sure you inform your host if you are bringing your own loader. It is the height of rudeness to leave this detail to the last minute or change the arrangement, as finding loaders is a big part of the host's or keeper's job. Informing a loader on a shoot day who has probably driven some distance to be there, that he is now not needed after all and must go on the flank or go beating, can be rather awkward.

Vehicles

Do specify in your letter if you would like your guests to bring a 4x4 vehicle, as many people have them but will not necessarily bring them unless asked. With fuel prices so high, they may opt to bring a different car. You don't want to end up having to hire or borrow an extra vehicle.

If your guests will be arriving by train or plane, you might need to offer to provide their cartridges. Remember to ask them which bore they need. As a guest, it is very important that you remember to pay for these. To avoid any awkwardness, just stuff some cash in a named envelope and leave it in the gun-room, saying who it is from.

Make contact and be enthusiastic!

The onus is on the guest to make contact with his host a few days before the shoot date, and NOT the other way round. Your host will be quite busy enough firming up arrangements with the keeper, or shoot agent, the lunch lady, and so on, to be calling all eight Guns up. So it really is up to you to make a quick telephone call to confirm everything, especially as it may have been three months or more since the invitation was issued. It is polite to call or e-mail anyway, so that you can express some enthusiasm about the day. An enthusiastic guest is gratifying to any host, who could by now be suffering pre-shoot nerves.

When you call to confirm the arrangements, it is best not to ask how many

'*...and then he comes downstairs, wearing plus-fours and carrying a gun...*'

cartridges to bring, or who is going to be there; this is like asking what you are having for dinner and who is coming when invited to a dinner party.

I have never thought it matters much whether you put in a whole box of 250 cartridges in the boot of your car, or just 100. Assuming you are driving to the shoot and not going by train, it really makes no odds to just slide in a slab of 250. (Don't forget, by the way, that you will need to show your gun licence when you go to buy your cartridges.) Always take more than you think you will use. Running short of cartridges can be deemed rather rude, as if you are not expecting much of a day. In the past shoot owners would have sent you home for such an impertinence!

Invitation Dos and Don'ts

Always reply to invitations promptly

If you have to refuse, do so immediately

If you are in any doubt at all about your availability, refuse

Never cancel just because a better invitation has come your way

Make sure you know the exact location of the shoot and leave enough time to get there safely and on time

Don't overwhelm a guest with too many dates

Don't wait for your host to contact you nearer the date: you should contact him first

Never accept an invitation to shoot from someone you know you will never want to invite back

Do try to invite your host back if you accept an invitation

If you are planning a shoot yourself, send out the invitations well in advance

Do make all arrangements absolutely clear, preferably in writing, stating date, venue, arrival time, and if the invitation includes an overnight stay

---

2
The Shooting House Party

'A shooting house party is like Christmas, without all the b******s'

There is nothing more enjoyable than a shooting house party. Not only do you have the luxury of merely rolling out of bed and trundling down for breakfast to be in the right place, you have all the fun of being away from home, which is like a mini-holiday in itself. More often than not, a marvellous dinner is laid on too, sometimes formal, sometimes less so. As a good friend was once heard to observe, 'A shooting house party is like Christmas, without all the bollocks!' You have the pleasure of being amongst friends, with loads of delicious food and flowing wine, in a wonderfully spoiling and exciting environment, as you look forward to, or reflect on, the day's sport. A lifelong friendship may well develop from a chance meeting at a shooting party.

The packing

The only drawback about being invited to a shooting house party is the packing. You need simply enormous amounts of kit. Not only do you have to remember the stuff for the shoot day itself, but also the appropriate outfit for the Saturday night – is it black tie or jeans 'n' heels? On Sunday morning, will it be smart or casual? By the time you've finished packing, found the place, unpacked (or worse, had your bags unpacked for you, which can be very embarrassing – ask Cherie Blair) you need to get into party mode.

Party on down

Shooting house parties can be quite raucous affairs. Alcohol and anticipation can be a powerful combination and can have quite a dramatic effect on people. I have danced the conga on the rooftops at midnight in Suffolk, played endless games of Sardines in various houses and hotels across the land, and in Hertfordshire one New Year all the men in the party decided to go skinny-dipping in the lake and then we played Murder in the Dark. What with hilarious games of charades and corridor-creeping antics amongst the singles, shooting house parties are always fabulously entertaining. The knock-on effect of all this ribaldry is that the next day you feel you're amongst friends, even if you've only met them the night before. You are expected to sing for your supper, so do join in the merriment: don't be a wallflower, or an atmosphere-hoover. On the other hand, don't stay up all night drinking your host's bottle of house-present whisky! Once he (or she) turns in for the night, then that is your signal to go to bed too.

There are, of course, a few other things about shooting house parties which, as the perfect guest, you need to know.

Maggie Wyvill, who with her husband, Charles, hosts shooting parties at local shoots from their Yorkshire home most days of the season, sent me this amusing poem when I asked her for some stories about guests behaving badly. It is called *The Perfect Pest* and Maggie wishes she could have this poem embroidered on a pillow to put in certain guests' rooms!

'She merely sent a wire to say
That she was coming down to stay.
She brought a maid of minxome look
Who promptly quarrelled with the cook.
She smoked and dropped with ruthless hand
Hot ashes on the Steinway grand.
She strode across the parquet floors
In hobnailed boots from out of doors
She said the water wasn't hot
And Jane gave notice on the spot.
She kept her bell in constant peals
And never was in time for meals.
And, when at last, with joyful heart
We thrust her in the luggage cart,
In half an hour, she came again and said
"My dear, I've missed the train".'

Timing

Firstly, it's a good idea to arrive at the time you say you will. You are usually invited before dinner, around 6pm, which gives you time to change if necessary. Don't be tempted to arrive any earlier in case your host is not ready for you. There may well be a shoot that day too and you will be barging into the shoot tea. As a rule, most

'He'll never know. He went to bed HOURS ago...'

hosts don't like the team of departing Guns running into the new arrivals. Also they will appreciate a bit of a rest between guests leaving and new ones arriving. So don't be early.

Guns in the house straight away

Make sure you bring your guns into the house straight away and keep them in your room unless there is a gunroom you can use. Many a guest has been lulled into a false sense of security thinking that because he's parked in a private driveway, his car is safe. One guest, arriving for some grouse shooting at Reeth, in his excitement left his car keys in the door of his car in the car park of the pub where we were all staying.

A while later, once the 'hellos' and introductions were over, he realised to his horror that his car had been stolen. Worse than the fact that there were about 500 12-bore cartridges on board, was that his two labradors were inside the car. These weren't just any labradors either – he regarded them almost as his children; they had been bridesmaids at his wedding and slept on his bed each night. Luckily, there was a happy ending to the story and the dogs were found, safe and sound, in another stolen car, a few miles away!

No dogs in the house

Don't automatically expect to bring your gundog into the house. Always ask permission from your host well ahead of time. Just because the place is crawling with dogs doesn't mean that yours will be welcome! A good guest will leave his dog in his car, or if there are kennels provided, ask to use one of them.

A guest of mine staying in my small cottage in Lincolnshire asked if his labrador could sleep in the little porch which also served as the coat and wellie area. It was quite a cold night and he was worried that his dog would get too cold left in the car. I knew he'd rather have had his dog on his bed but I didn't want to be finding dog hairs in the laundry for months, so the dog stayed in the porch and made a hell of a racket, howling all night. By the next morning he had chewed his way through three shooting coats…

Another friend of mine had someone to stay who was accompanied by a very strong golden labrador with bags of character. Known for chewing and ruining furniture as well as the interiors of cars, the dog needed somewhere really 'safe' for the night. He was duly put in the somewhat spartan 'freezer room'. During the night he somehow managed to eat his way *through* the door and got into the main part of the house!

Dogs can be quite handy allies though. Someone I know was staying in a house party for a shoot in Northumberland. He takes up the story:

'I'd had too many whiskies, and decided to retire to bed, feeling the worse for

The dogs' welcome

wear. As I was getting some air on the front steps, there was a quickening in the tummy department. Suddenly I knew I was going to have to "go" right there on the lawn behind the vehicles. The next morning my hostess was glaring at the lawn saying "What f*****g dog has done that?" I replied innocently: "Sometimes my dog has tummy problems when he travels…"'

Nigel Hawkins, fanatical and deadly grouse shot (who in 2008 shot over sixty days on grouse alone) was staying with a party at a hotel in the Yorkshire Dales before a day's shooting at Gunnerside. He'd stayed up until 3am chatting up the barmaid and overslept badly. When he got to the dining-room everyone else was already tucking into their full English breakfast. He says:

'The hotel staff told me there'd be no time for me to have a cooked breakfast, so I went to my car where I had a very sweet young lab bitch and got a clean dog bowl. I went back to the breakfast room and told a story about having no breakfast for my dog. Naturally, all the dog lovers put in a sausage, or a bit of bacon, or some fried egg and so on. They were furious when I then sat down to eat it out of the dog bowl! They would never have shared their breakfast with *me*!'

Be prepared for odd customs

Shooting can present a minefield of problems and embarrassments – and not just when you're out there pulling the trigger. House parties and shoot dinners are in a league of their own. Mike Barnes, editor of *Fieldsports* magazine tells me about an extraordinary house party he once attended with his wife.

'As with most things in life it is always better to know where you stand. Times have changed but it remains a fact that wives or girlfriends are not always welcome. I remember taking Mrs B to a shoot in East Anglia. The day was good, our host benevolent and there was every reason to look forward to dinner at his house afterwards. One slight technical hitch – the gin and tonics were followed by a request from said host for Mrs B to join the children watching television elsewhere in the house whilst us chaps had our supper. I say "us chaps" but in fact we were also joined by the host's lover! His wife was with the children. It was not an evening that had a happy ending.'

It's not always the hosts who behave badly. A friend told me about an amusing incident at a house party in Norfolk a few years ago.

'I was invited to an early season partridge day. Our hostess had just had a new deep pile carpet laid in the hall, of which she was very proud. Unfortunately for her, the gardener had left the mower under the porch and the guests all got so drunk that evening, that one of them thought it would be a laugh to mow it!'

No one was very popular the next day!

Presents for your hosts

'Take your hostess a nice present – she might influence the next invitation,' suggests Ralph Northumberland. Also, a good bottle or something well thought out for your host is always a good idea. If you feel awkward giving these, or the right moment doesn't arise, just leave them in the hall with a note attached.

Be nice to the staff and helpful to your host

If it's a grand house party, there may well be several indoor staff. John Morgan writes in *Debrett's New Guide to Etiquette & Modern Manners*:

'It is important to be polite and friendly to staff at all times, and to remember that they are professionals in their sphere. Those unused to servants sometimes behave in a way that causes embarrassment all round: too haughtily, too chummily or too apologetically.'

If it is a less formal household, then help your host if he is organising dinner himself: try to make yourself useful by helping to clear the plates, or bringing in the next course.

The morning after...

Make sure you have set your alarm clock so that you don't oversleep the next morning, and appear at breakfast only after you have seen to your dog. That means taking it on the lead somewhere well away from the front lawn.

Shoot breakfasts

Breakfasts on shoot days tend not to be particularly formal. You will be told what time it will be served and you need to be there as on time as you can manage, particularly if you know you are going to have a full cooked breakfast. If you're just a coffee and cornflakes person, you don't have to be as punctual as all that. Conversation is usually sparse and most people keep their noses in their newspapers. It's not considered at all rude just to sit down, eat, and get up and go when you've finished, regardless of what others are doing.

If your partner is not joining you until lunchtime, there is no need for her (or him) to come down for the shoot breakfast and most hosts make this quite clear the night before. There is often a later sitting. In some houses the ladies are lucky enough to get breakfast in bed.

Clear your room and tipping

It is a good idea to pack your things if you are leaving after shooting, so your room can be made ready for the next lot of guests. You also need to remember to tip the staff before you leave, preferably before you go out shooting that morning.

All the people who have looked after you should be tipped, such as the cleaner, whom you no doubt won't have seen, but who has obviously contributed to your comfort. The easiest thing to do is to leave an appropriate amount in your room. A quick word with your host or hostess will clarify this.

Take your belongings with you!

Try not to leave any kit behind when you leave. It is highly inconvenient for your host to have to track down something you have left behind and post it back to you. If you tend to be absent-minded, it might be a good idea to sew some children's style nametapes into all your favourite shooting jackets. Then at least you stand some chance of finding them at the end of the day.

Try not to leave any kit behind

Leave promptly after tea

If you are leaving after shooting, don't linger too long after tea. Your host might be expecting another lot of guests, and anyway he probably needs some time to unwind after what was no doubt an exhausting day for him.

If staying the whole weekend

If you are invited to spend another night after shooting you are very lucky indeed. There is nothing nicer than relaxing after the day's sport rather than driving home in the dark for hours with a car full of kit to be unloaded, gun to be cleaned, birds to deal with before you can even dream of having a hot bath and dinner.

Inform your host of your plans

Your host will no doubt have informed you if you are expected to stay for Sunday lunch or not. Mostly this is assumed to be the case and your host will have catered for you accordingly. If for whatever reason you know in advance that you won't be able to stay for lunch, you need to make this known rather than just announcing it on the day at breakfast. This is just good manners.

Don't lie in too long

Depending on the sort of house party it is, you will know roughly what time you need to stagger downstairs for breakfast, but don't sleep in too long if you suspect that no one else will. In some houses you can't expect breakfast at 11am, while in others, it's fine and you'll just be making your own toast and tea. You have to gauge each situation differently.

Leave by 3pm on Sunday

But one thing that doesn't alter, regardless of how formal or casual the house party, is that a good guest is expected to leave after lunch and not hang around all Sunday afternoon. Your host and hostess need a chance to clear up and relax and have a little post-shooting post-mortem after you've gone. The old saying about guests and fish really does hold true – 'guests are like fish, they go off after three days' – so don't outstay your welcome!

3
On Arriving

*'I arrived at the shoot on time, said my "hellos", opened the boot and there
was my strimmer, but no gun. I'd left it at home!'*
William Garfit, artist, writer and renowned shot

I f you are not lucky enough to be staying as a guest the night before, then you must allow plenty of time to get to the shoot. This is very important, both for you and the host. Being late is incredibly stressful for all concerned – not only will it spoil your focus and concentration for the first drive and probably beyond, it will be intensely irritating for your host and oh, around forty others, if you count beaters, pickers-up, and fellow Guns. You simply must not be late.

As I have said, if you live more than two hours away, aim to stay as near to the shoot as possible to reduce the potential for bad traffic delays or getting lost. Allow far more time than you think you need, and if you end up sitting in your car reading the paper for twenty minutes, it's still a lot more relaxing than sweating away in traffic or lost down some country lane to nowhere. Mobile phones don't always work in rural areas either, so you cannot rely on yours to announce your tardiness. Equally, though, if you arrive more than fifteen minutes early, don't ring the bell to your host's house and expect him to be pleased to see you! Your early arrival will almost certainly be more of an irritation than a joy as he will no doubt be frantically rushing about tying up loose ends and preparing for the day. Getting you a cup of coffee will not be high on his list of priorities. Just stay in your vehicle, relax and read the paper for a while.

OLIVER PRESTON

Allow plenty of time

If thick snow is on the ground on the morning of the shoot, or if there is a total white-out of fog, it might be a good idea to call the host to check if the day is cancelled. In any other kind of extreme weather, such as storms, gale-force winds or torrential rain, you should assume the shoot is still going ahead unless you are told otherwise. Naturally you should allow even more time than normal to reach the shoot in such conditions.

When the host says, 'We will meet at 9.15 and move off at 9.30', that is what he means. Aim to be there at 9am or at the latest 9.10am. If you arrive at 9.30am your lateness will affect the whole team, who won't have been able to do the draw for numbers without you. You should apologise profusely and not delay the draw any further by messing about with your kit. If you arrive later than half an hour after the meeting time, be warned: it is considered quite normal for everyone to carry on, leaving you to make your own way to the line. If you are lucky someone will have been left behind to direct you, but many hosts do not do this, judging it better to teach the latecomer a good lesson.

Many people do cut it too fine to get to a shoot, which can have disastrous consequences. The following story shows more than anything how even the best of plans can be turned upside down by a combination of red tape and bad luck. Only sheer determination and charm got this particular Gun to the shoot at all.

Julia Plumptre, then known as Julia Proudfoot, who was a co-founder of *Country Illustrated*, had an interesting time getting to a shoot on the Isle of Islay. The rest of the party, guests of Sir John Mactaggart, had travelled the day before, but due to work commitments Julia had planned to arrive on the shoot day itself. She was scheduled to travel from Heathrow on the first flight, changing at Glasgow for the Islay plane and arriving just in time for the second drive. Julia felt perfectly prepared, travelling in her best cashmere shooting suit and with her gun packed in her suitcase to save time. At that time this was permissible on domestic flights.

Suffice to say that all Julia's plans went awry. Her ticket was found to be invalid so she had to buy a new one, which delayed her; because she was late her luggage could no longer go in the hold, which meant that she was almost arrested for having a shotgun in her hand luggage… She missed her plane but caught the next one. However she was then stranded at Glasgow airport, with no hope of a connecting flight to Islay due to the stormy weather. Still undeterred, the indomitable Julia cleverly unearthed the pilot of a small seaplane and begged him to fly her to Islay.

'It was very wild indeed, we were like a leaf in the wind. It was just like being on a bucking horse. We couldn't land at the airport, it was far too rough. The pilot asked: "Do you know where this place is?" and after a couple of fly-bys we found it, swooped down and landed in the bay just across from Sir John's house.'

By now the guests had assembled in the dining-room for lunch and Lady Mactaggart noticed the sun was reflecting oddly off the sea. 'There's a plane in the bay!' she exclaimed and two of the party, including Sir John, took out a rowing boat to see what had befallen the little aircraft. To everyone's surprise, as they reached the plane the cockpit opened and a tweed-clad leg and a Gucci heel appeared. They couldn't believe their eyes. But there was no warm welcome for Proudfoot, all she got was: 'Quick! For God's sake get in the bloody boat, Proudfoot! It's got a leak, we're going to sink!' So her adventure wasn't quite over, but Julia did manage to shoot three drives in the afternoon and also provided a memorable entry in Sir John's game book.

You might have heard another story of a Gun running late, arriving at the meeting point to find it deserted, and then spotting a team of Guns lined up in a field close by. He parks hastily on the verge, gets out his gun and takes his place on the vacant peg he assumed had been left for him. Blazing away, having a great time, it isn't until the Duke of Marlborough comes striding up to him at the end of the drive asking who the bloody hell he is, that he realises he has joined the wrong line of Guns!

Nick Wilson, a friend, told me the other day about a Gun who kept everyone waiting at his father's shoot in the Borders. It was a freezing cold day and the driveway to the house was covered in a glaze of ice. The Guns were standing around, waiting for him. When the latecomer saw everyone gathered together, he sped down the drive, lost control on the ice and skidded straight into the side of another guest's smart 4x4 vehicle. Nick's father, Lynn, didn't bat an eyelid. He just said 'Ah, hello, Bob, now I don't believe you've met Fred Smith…', whose car it was that he'd just smashed into.

Travelling by train

If travelling by train, it's safer and easier to travel with your gun in a special gun case rather than in its gun slip which could alarm the general public. These are widely available and with any luck people will think you are transporting a musical instrument rather than a lethal weapon.

One poor friend of ours was actually arrested and removed from the train on his way up to Edinburgh because a member of the public alerted the police to him having a gun. The rest of the party travelling with him had rather sensibly taken their guns apart and had placed theirs in their luggage.

Bring a present!

Assuming you've managed to get to the shoot on time and not smashed into anyone else's car, one more thing to remember is that it's a good idea to bring a present for your host. Neither traditional nor expected, a thoughtful present nevertheless makes you stand out from the crowd, and sets you well on the way to becoming a perfect guest.

Don't forget your gun...

Another important point may seem obvious: bring the right kit with you. A major nuisance to any shoot host is for a guest to start the day by asking if he can borrow this or that because he's forgotten something. We will consider all the essentials in a moment, but first a cautionary tale. A few seasons ago, Will Garfit committed a heinous crime. He takes up the story:

'It was the first day of the season, I'd been busy polishing my cartridge bag and gun slip so I had everything ready for the next day. I'd even taken the gun out of the cabinet, it was all ready on the studio table. In the morning, I had a few errands to do on the way to the shoot so I left in plenty of time. I had to drop somthing off and pick up a garden strimmer. I arrived at the shoot on time, said my "hellos", opened the boot and there was the strimmer, but no gun. I'd left it at home! Friends all wound me up, saying it wasn't particularly complimentary to my host's partridges that I'd left my gun at home and brought my strimmer instead!'

Luckily for Will, the gun he borrowed proved to be his lucky charm as he managed to be in the shooting all day and got far more than his share of the bag!

The right kit

It has never been so easy to acquire really good shooting kit. Whether by mail order, internet shopping, shooting school outlets or specialist shooting shops, there is a huge choice. Remember, though, that comfort and practicality are key. Nothing you wear

'Yo babe! I'm on the tube.'

for shooting should stop you from mounting the gun unencumbered, or from swinging easily and certainly nothing should impede your vision. Your clothing and accessories should feel right and look the part. Some of the clothing for driven shooting is quite specialised and you may not own a pair of plus fours. Cord trousers are fine, but do bear in mind that plus fours are the most practical and comfortable option, particularly if worn with wellies. Here are a few pointers, to help you in your quest to find the right kit.

The shooting jacket

Probably the most important and most expensive of all the items you will need is the shooting jacket. Some people believe there is no such thing as the perfect shooting jacket: many Guns buy several before they settle on their final choice, or use different ones for different weather conditions. Most are Gore-Tex lined and will protect you from both the rain and the cold and will also have perfect pockets from which to load. The problem with many tweed jackets is that they are too warm for early season days. So it's a good idea to invest in a sleeveless, i.e. waistcoat type, which also needs good wide pockets for loading from, as well as proper shoulder padding. These are available in many different fabrics, including tweed or cotton canvas.

Another vital item is a very lightweight, breathable, 'shell' of a waterproof jacket for those days when it really pours down with rain. This should be large enough to wear over several layers and should also have suitable pockets to load from. Ideally, it won't rustle like an anorak either! A rain jacket incorporating all these qualities is very hard to find, but Schöffel, Barbour and Musto, amongst others, make very good ones.

Plus fours

What we routinely refer to as plus fours are in fact plus twos, the 'two' referring to the inches of fabric extending below the knee. They come in tweed, moleskin, corduroy, loden, nubuck and cotton canvas. Many people favour tweed because of its hard-wearing qualities; if it is your choice too, there is no need to add a matching jacket and/or waistcoat to your plus fours – you could be mistaken for the keeper, because they are usually the only ones who still wear three-piece shooting suits of the estate tweed. Mixing and matching of tweeds is completely acceptable as long as the two don't clash too much.

Thermals and shirts

Most shooting shirts tend to be the cream-coloured country check ones, known as Tattersalls, worn either with or without a tie. You could also invest in some more muted coloured shirts such as moss or beige for warmer days, when you might shoot in shirtsleeves and a Tattersall shirt would be too bright and visible to the birds.

On cold days, layering is the answer. Some of the best shots wear several thin layers rather than fewer, thicker ones. I would recommend several finest silk under-shirts or polo necks which you can get from companies such as Orvis, which specialises in thermal underwear. Thermal or silk long johns are also a good idea when the temperature plummets.

Sweaters/fleeces

These days people will often wear a fleece instead of a traditional wool sweater. Warm, easily washable, light and not vulnerable to moths, they are the most practical addition to any shooting person's wardrobe. But if it's a very formal lunch, a smart lambswool 'V' neck in the usual palette of beige, browns or greens which could go under a jacket is just the thing.

Ties

People have strong views on ties. Some Guns always wear them, feeling that they should 'honour' the birds. Others hate them, finding them too constrictive. It's a personal thing. For smart driven days, you cannot go wrong if you wear a tie: the usual style is to wear a woollen one or a knitted silk, or one from a pro-shooting organisation. On the plus side, wearing a tie keeps the draughts out, and it can also be useful if you lose your dog lead, or if you need to make a splint for any broken bones!

Shooting socks

This is the one area where you can risk a bit of colour. Some Guns favour red or blue or purple or even orange – anything goes. Contrasting patterns at the top in checkerboard design or with knitted catchphrases such as 'Bloody' on one sock and 'Dog!' on the other were very popular, but are perhaps a bit passé now.

Footwear

Walking boots: If it is dry underfoot, a pair of walking boots is ideal, particularly on rugged terrain where a good grip is essential. On grouse moors in particular they are recommended, as there can be a lot of walking, usually uphill, when a normal wellie-boot won't quite do the job. On the moor walking boots are more comfortable when worn with gaiters, such as those worn by ramblers, to avoid getting bits of scratchy heather embedded in your woollen shooting socks.

Wellington boots: Aim to get yourself the best wellies you can afford as this will save you from years of cold feet. The warmest ones are neoprene-lined; those shaped to your foot which give your ankle good support are much better than basic unlined ones. On a cold day's pheasant shooting in January you will be thankful you splashed out! Le Chameau, Aigle and Hunter all make fabulous boots, some with zips, others with just a top strap. Perhaps the most luxurious boot of the moment is the leather Dubarry boot which is extremely popular these days. As comfortable as a walking boot, these are leather throughout and are completely waterproof.

Gloves

The wearing of gloves is a very personal preference. Some Guns loathe them, finding them cumbersome and annoying and will only wear them on the coldest of days whilst others find them invaluable. Gloves can also be useful for big days when barrels get hot, so that you don't burn your hands: although if you are shooting with a side-by-side you can use a hand guard to prevent this. At the other extreme, having very cold hands can be dangerous out shooting as you can lose dexterity and make a mistake with safety catches or triggers.

As with everything shooting-related, you need several different pairs for different weather conditions. Leather gloves, whilst being tough and flexible, should ideally fit your hands like a second skin enabling you to load without fumbling. However, leather gloves are hopeless in the rain as they quickly get sodden and your hands will get very cold. Of course on a really wet day you could take five pairs of leather ones and have a dry pair each drive.

Scarves

On the whole, large bulky scarves are not a good idea out shooting as they can interfere with how you mount your gun. To be recommended, though, are the special shooting cravats, traditionally towelling but also fleece, which are very good at keeping the draughts and the rain out. They even keep you warm when they are rain-soaked.

Headgear

The choice is endless, but overwhelmingly the flat cap seems to have remained the most popular headgear. At least you can wear your ear defenders over the top comfortably. Some prefer the 'pork pie' hat but either is useful for keeping the sun – or the rain – out of your eyes. The one problem with a flat cap is that it does not keep your ears warm.

A trilby or a German Alpine hat is fine for a still day, but a strong wind will whip it away. Also you cannot wear your ear defenders over the brim of a hat like this. On a really cold day, you could do a lot worse than turn up with a woolly hat, in a suitably dull colour, which will keep you very warm (especially your ears), won't blow off and will still enable you to don your ear defenders. Baseball caps are not really acceptable, even tweed ones, especially on a formal shoot. Hoods are not ideal either, except in a real downpour, as they restrict your view severely which means you miss seeing the birds on your extreme left or right.

Vital equipment

Your gun: We've said this before: whatever you do, don't forget it!

Cartridges: Always take more than you expect to use and make sure they are the right bore for your gun.

Gun sleeve: You simply cannot turn up to a formal driven day without a gun sleeve. The best ones are made of leather lined with sheepskin and zip all the way down. Buy a good quality one as it will really protect your gun from the rigours of a shoot day. The flimsy ones with no lining are just not up to the job of protecting your gun properly.

Cartridge bag: A cartridge bag is another vital piece of kit. The perfect cartridge bag will be made of strong leather, with a fully hinged flap to make a wide opening so that even your gloved hand can load from it quickly. It should last you a lifetime so it is a worthwhile investment. Your initials on the front will avoid any panicky cartridge bag mix-ups which could scupper your drive or someone else's.

Ear protection: Whether you wear your ear protection inside your ear as an earplug, or over your ear, as a pair of ear defenders, depends entirely on you. Some people prefer earplugs whilst others maintain that the sound is absorbed not just inside the ear, but all around the ear and that the best form of protection is a pair of ear defenders, which covers the whole ear.

If you choose earplugs, there is a type to suit every pocket, from the cheapest foam disposable ones to the most expensive electronic earplugs, specially moulded to your ear. However, these tiny gadgets are spectacularly easy to lose and very expensive to replace. You could opt for a pair which mould to the ear because they are flexible; they are not battery-operated, but contain a special sonic valve. This type is not hugely expensive. At least with any earplug you can wear a hat with a brim, which can have its own advantages.

For those Guns who prefer ear defenders worn over the ears, the bog standard ones work fine but can be a bit disorientating as they muffle all sounds, including the birds' wing beat and the whistle at the end of the drive. However, you can buy special electronic ones which allow you to hear everything in perfect pitch – all the sounds of the drive, as well as any conversation (even from the next door butt) yet totally muffle the sound of the gun being fired. The only disadvantage of these is that they are spectacularly easy to leave switched on by mistake, so flat batteries are par for the course.

Finally, you could choose solar-powered ear defenders, which are a great alternative to battery-guzzling electronic ones. The marketing spiel insists that they work even on dull, cloudy days, which is just as well!

Safety specs: On the whole these tend to be worn when grouse or partridge shooting, but the experts recommend that they should always be worn on the shooting field, as well as for clay pigeon shooting. Available with clear lenses or with various tints, a good pair will have protective side guards as well so that your whole eye is covered.

Waterproof trousers: You should never arrive at a shoot without a pair of these. There is nothing worse than being absolutely soaked through in the first drive of the day and having to endure the damp and cold all day. Try to get ones which have zips from hem to calf to help you get them on and off easily over your boots.

Other useful items: Shooting stick, thumb stick, hill bag, travelling gun cleaning kit; knife, binoculars, chocolate, hip flask, midge spray, sun cream; water, for you and for your dog; an extra dog lead; spares of gloves, hats and ear defenders, just in case.

When you pack for a shoot day or a shooting house party, you must be prepared for every eventuality and for every kind of weather. It is no good having all the right kit if you have left half of it at home.

One final point to bear in mind – when you arrive at a shoot, do ensure that your wellington boots are not covered in mud from your last foray. This not only gives a very bad impression but can also spread infection from one part of the country to another.

Clean kit

The same goes for your waterproof trousers – try to remember to brush them off or wash them after your day out.

Introductions...

When you arrive at the shoot, if there are other Guns already there, get out of your car and greet them, don't wait to be introduced. Shooting is a social sport and as hard as it may be to break the ice with total strangers, it must be done. Small talk about your journey and where you live and so on, is all part and parcel of the day's sport. Don't spend too long messing around in the car, or, worst sin of all, sitting there chatting on your mobile phone as you wait for the draw. Many shots firmly believe that mobile phones should be banned from shoots except in emergencies. Some hosts will fine you every time they see you using yours!

One shoot host felt so strongly about this that when he was running a day up in Yorkshire, where a guest was permanently on his phone between drives, he decided to teach him a lesson. After the mid-morning drink the Gun was still so absorbed on the phone that the shoot host led the other Guns to the next drive, leaving him behind. The drive started without him. He would have been in the middle of the line, on a very good drive. When he caught up, the Gun was furious, whereupon the host merely said, 'Oh, we didn't want to disturb you, you seemed so engrossed in your call'.

Your host

When your host first appears on the day, make sure you greet him straight away. It is very rude to expect him to come and seek you out first. Say how thrilled you are to be there, but be mindful of the fact that he probably can't chat to you for too long. If you stay nearby, you may get the chance to hear a few of the introductions again: trying to memorise eight names almost simultaneously when all the guns look identical in their green shooting jackets and flat caps is very hard! Repeating names as you are introduced may help you to keep them in mind. It's quite handy to know at least your neighbouring Guns' names in case you need to get their attention later on, as in: 'Charles! Over!' or 'I've picked one of yours, Rupert!'

42

Don't always expect there to be seven or eight other Guns shooting. Some hosts prefer to keep things intimate and might shoot with just two or three of you in the line. Fanatical shot John Plumptre occasionally enjoys inviting just one other guest to his shoot, Chetney Marshes, and loves to see the look on people's faces as they realise there are no other guests.

Make sure you also introduce yourself to the keeper or shoot agent if they are still around. Similarly, when you see the beaters for the first time, say a general and jovial good morning to them too.

One last check

A quick final check ensures that you have your essential kit: gun, cartridge bag, gloves and ear defenders. Quickly assemble your gun if it has been in a travelling case. If it's looking ominously like rain, it is a good idea to put on your waterproofs straight away as a good drenching in the first drive will mean you'll be damp the whole day and probably leave a wet patch on the dining room chairs at lunch...

All this kit is easy to mislay, so a lightweight canvas kit bag or hill bag which you can sling over your shoulder will keep everything together, so that you don't reach your peg lacking some vital piece of equipment.

The draw

Once everyone is assembled and your host is about to offer round the pegs for the draw (or playing cards, or numbered shot glasses) make sure you are in the right place, i.e. close to your host and not busy fiddling with your cartridges in the back of your car, and keep quiet for a moment. It is usual for the host to turn to the Gun standing on his left and offer to him first, and then proceed clockwise around the circle of Guns. Do not jostle for your turn, just wait for the pegs to be offered to you.

My brother, Charles Nickerson (a demon grouse shot), has written a short piece about the ritual and protocol of the draw from which he has kindly allowed me to quote a section entitled, *How complicated can a number possibly be?*

'You will each be invited to extract a sliver of precious metal or other material from the proffered position finder on which you should eventually perceive an often-indecipherable hieroglyphic representing your "number". Position finders come in many designs, shapes and sizes but are always treasured possessions. This number will be hidden from view as you take your pick. There is a gambler in all of us and at this moment you will hope that fortune will favour your choice.

'In the flurry of the excitement of the draw, coupled with the need to return said sliver to your host's palm, whilst everyone will be surreptitiously attempting to establish your number, it is amazing how a fog may well descend over you and dissolve your brain cells to the point of removing the selected number from

The draw

wherever in your brain you intended to store it. This is caused by a variety of emotions taking hold all at once, not the least of which is the terror or pleasure of discovering between whom you will have drawn to stand each drive.

'It is a useful tip, therefore, to make an extra effort to remember your number and also share it with your loader as soon as possible because he for one will certainly not forget, even if he makes it obvious you did not choose a number to his liking in relation to the chosen beat and which butts will attract the most shooting…

'Your host will involve his guests in calculus by saying (something like), "we number from the right" or "the left" or "from the bottom of the hill" and "move up two" or "three" or even "one", or even "odd numbers up and even numbers down after each drive". This is where we find out just how complicated a number can be…'

The safety drill

Just before the draw or just after, the host or shoot organiser will give a little talk, or 'safety drill'. He will normally tell you what you will be shooting, for example, 'Today we'll be shooting partridge and pheasant' or 'Today we will be shooting cocks only'. So it's vital that you listen carefully to save major embarrassment later. He may also say things like 'Wait for the horn to start' or 'Start shooting when you get to your peg' or 'No pigeons before the partridges'. Occasionally the instructions are more complicated, such as 'Only shoot a hen if you have shot a cock bird first' or, very confusingly, 'Only shoot the red legs, you must not shoot the English greys', which fills most Guns with dread lest they get it wrong…

If any aspect of the instructions is confusing to you, now is the time to seek clarification! If your host has specifically said not to shoot pigeons, or woodcock, then for heaven's sake respect his wishes, even if you privately disagree. Remember: when you are out shooting, it's a bit like joining the army for the day, and you must show absolute deference to your host and the keeper. You should obey their instructions without question.

Safety will also be discussed, which is obviously a serious concern. For this reason you will be told in 99 cases out of 100, 'absolutely no ground game'. There are occasionally some exceptions to this. If a fox comes out of a wood, some hosts would be furious if you didn't try and shoot it: others would send you home if you did!

Take some bismuth cartridges

When shooting somewhere new, it is a good idea to take the proper cartridges for wildfowl, just in case your host slips in a duck drive. Bismuth is now the legal requirement for any wildfowl, including snipe. If you shoot a snipe on a grouse moor, legally you are supposed to use a bismuth cartridge because a snipe is part of the wader family. If you make a mistake and shoot one with a normal lead cartridge, then you should take the bird home to eat, to avoid it having to go to a game dealer where checks could be made. The estate could then get into trouble for your inadvertent error.

Travelling around the shoot

You now need to find out if you are taking your own vehicle, or piling into a gun-wagon. Not all shoots have gun-buses or gun-wagons any more. The days of tractors and trailers with straw bales to sit on are long gone because of the health and safety laws governing passengers. You now need to offer something a little more substantial which is safer. Huge Bedford vans make for great shoot vehicles, even if you need a ladder to get up into them. There is something rather fun about the whole team travelling around the shoot together: what you lack in comfort is more than made up for by the sense of bonhomie. It is not just more friendly, it is more eco-friendly too. If you arrive at a shoot where everyone is decamping into one of these vehicles, it is very bad form to refuse. You must be prepared to forego the leather-lined interior of your car and say, 'Of course, I'd be delighted'. Privately you may be fuming at the thought of leaving your precious cocoon, filled with kit and comforts, to sit hugger-mugger with everyone else. The ride will be bumpy, at least two people will be smoking (and maybe pipes at that), and dogs may well try to lick your face or mount your leg, all the way round the shoot. Just put up with it!

If there is no gun-bus and you haven't got your own 4x4 vehicle, you could ask your host or a fellow Gun if you could hop in with them. Bear in mind that if you have a dog, a child or partner with you, it is more courteous to bring your own vehicle

'Now that the children have gone back to school, the wife really enjoys some quality time with me.'

rather than just assume there will be space for them too. It's a good idea to warn your host if you won't be bringing a suitable vehicle so that he can work out the logistics of getting around the shoot.

It is the height of rudeness to turn up with a 4x4 vehicle and then refuse to take it on the shoot. I recently witnessed just this – the owner said that he couldn't bear to have anyone's muddy boots messing up the interior of his vehicle which he used all week for work. Everyone then had to pile into the back of only one Land Rover! So if you do have your own 4x4, be prepared at all times to accommodate guests in your car, and welcome them graciously. Expect dogs, small children on occasions, and make the necessary arrangements to clear a space in the boot for the dog and the rear seat for any potential passengers. Remember to ensure that any guns in the boot are safely stowed so that no visiting dog can jump up and tread on them, as this may break the stock. This can be a horribly costly mistake, as re-stocking starts at about £4,000…

I heard a story about a syndicate member at a shoot in Oxfordshire who was incredibly rude about sharing his vehicle. Most of the cars had already set off for the first drive when the shoot owner's elderly mother enquired of one of the Guns if she might have a lift to the first drive to watch the shooting.

'Sorry, no, I've got stuff on the back seat,' he replied as he drove off, leaving her to walk a mile to the first drive. Fortunately such behaviour is rare.

No boy-racers

It is polite to let the host's vehicle lead the way, so hang back a bit to allow him to do this, and just join in the convoy when you can. A good host will keep an eye on his rear-view mirror to make sure everyone is following, but you can lose a speedy host and then spend all morning trying to locate the shoot. Don't let this happen to you! Keep your wits about you and stick like glue to the car in front. Don't attempt any boy-racer tactics and just stay in single file, even if you are in what looks like a huge open field. No owner takes kindly to vehicles churning up his turf, or spoiling his setaside. Obviously if it's wet and the ground is boggy, go slowly, but don't stop or you may get stuck. Allow the car in front plenty of room if going up a hill.

An embarrassing moment

One day when Nick Wilson was in his twenties, he was organising the day at the family shoot in the Borders. On one drive, everyone was warned that a steep grassy bank would be very slippery and to take care going up it. Nick tells the story:

'The first vehicle went up, and then slid down the hill, getting bogged down in the middle of the field. The guest, Andrew Rettie, had to abandon it there, as there was no way he could move it without a tractor. So he got in with me. I said: "What you need is more speed, watch this." So I sped up the hill and almost got to the top, but then started to slide down it sideways, fast. There was nothing I could do. We went slap-bang into the side of poor Andrew's vehicle. It was the most embarrassing thing… but if it hadn't been there, I would probably have kept on going and ended up in the wood on the other side of the field!'

Car keys

These are always causing problems on shoot days. Friends of mine were invited to shoot at Belvoir Castle and planned to get a lift in another guest's Range Rover. They drove to his house in their little Nissan Micra and on arriving our friend realised he'd forgotten his shooting suit. Not wanting to delay their 'chauffeur', they told him to go on ahead without them while they went back home to retrieve the shooting suit. Arriving late and flustered at their hotel, as they hastily unpacked the car they somehow managed to lock the keys inside. The now desperate Gun picked up a brick and set about breaking into his own car. The first window he broke was useless as the car was on child-lock so he had to break another one – he had spotted the keys lying on the back flap of the boot. The enduring memory of him wriggling himself into the back of the car to retrieve them is enough to make me always think twice about where I put my car keys down!

What number was I again?

Hopefully by now you have not forgotten the peg number you drew, but if you have, you won't be the first person to do so. I have done it myself several times: there is such a lot to remember and think about, added to which is the stress of knowing that you will soon have to display to the world that you can actually shoot straight. It never ceases to amaze me how many top-ranking investment bankers who can do mathematical gymnastics in their heads with foreign exchange rates, interest rates and so on, just cannot fathom out which number they move up to after each drive.

One helpful hint is to make sure you identify the same neighbours as you started with as being on your left and right. Unless, that is, your host uses a system such as the Fairmile muddling system which is the system most favoured by Europeans who often like to have different neighbours on each side each drive. It really is a nightmare to remember where you are each drive, but luckily the system is very rarely used in the UK! Still, the number of people who stride merrily on past their peg does make for good entertainment.

If you are in difficulty, you could start by casually asking the Guns in your vehicle what their numbers are, and then by a process of elimination work out yours. If not, just 'fess up to your host and between you, you will get it right.

The first bird

Standing at your peg for the first drive can be very nerve-racking, even for experienced shots. You may be shooting on new ground, with new people, and more often than not your mind has not fully absorbed the pre-shoot chat about the day. So you stand there nervously facing the game coverts, not entirely sure if it's just pheasant or pheasant and partridge, or whether you should leave the partridge, or whether the partridge are wild greys and the host wants you to leave them or if he is one of the few to rear wild greys, in which case you *should* shoot them… All this can be very confusing.

Allied to the sense of anticipation is the dread that you may just not be on form, that for some reason you will miss every bird that flies over your head. As Daphne Hanbury says: 'If you shoot the first bird of the day, you never need to shoot another thing all day!' She's absolutely right of course, as everyone always sees and notices the very first bird of the day. This is why as you stand there, desperately hoping the first bird of the day *won't* fly over your head, you need to keep calm, keep focused and, according to the experts, concentrate on your footwork!

If you do miss the first few birds, it can make you very anxious and could set the tone for the entire day if you let it put you off your stride. The first drive, particularly when others may know that you perhaps haven't done as much shooting as they have, or if you are complete novice, these feelings of anxiety will be magnified. As long as you stay safe, that is the most important thing.

Pre-shoot nerves

Many Guns have admitted to me that quite often all this anticipation can have an unnerving effect on their bowels. One Gun, shooting grouse for the first time, suddenly had an urgent need to find a private moment alone before the beginning of the drive, so he wandered off into the distance to find a little dip in the heather.

Unfortunately this episode proved rather explosive and a fine pair of braces was irredeemably caught in the cross-fire. He abandoned them, and returned to his butt. Not only did he have to contend with some strange looks from his loader for having taken so long, but every time he raised his gun to take a shot, his plus fours started to slide down.

At the end of the drive, the beaters came in and he heard one say to another, 'By God, there's been a fox here!' 'Well', replied the other, 'I've never seen a fox wearing braces.'

4
Shooting Safely and Shooting Well

'If in doubt, don't shoot'
Jonathan Irby

The single most important thing to remember is to shoot safely. When you ask any shoot owner, keeper or organiser what is the most important thing about a team of Guns, safety is always at the top of the list. If a shooting accident occurs, it is the shoot organiser who is deemed to be at fault and who has to take the blame.

'You may be the greatest shot, but if you are unsafe, you won't be asked anywhere. You need not be the greatest shot, but if you are safe, you will be welcome everywhere,' says Jonathan Irby, general manager of the West London Shooting School (WLSS), and an instructor for many years. 'I tell any novice who's going to shoot game for the first time: "If you're in point-one per cent doubt, don't shoot".'

Most people taking up shooting today will not have had the advantage of a long country apprenticeship from childhood. However well a shooting school may have emphasised the concept of safety, putting it into practice on the field doesn't happen automatically. Fortunately for the beginner, there is usually someone experienced who can come and stand with you on the shoot, and it is a good idea to request this. Otherwise, Jonathan advises great caution at all times. He says: 'It's far better to have your host ask, "Why didn't you shoot at that?" rather than coming up to you saying: "Can I have a quiet word…".'

If you have never shot before, or are the slightest bit unsure of what to do, for goodness sake, tell your shoot host. There is absolutely no shame in doing so and everyone will respect you far more for being honest than for pretending you actually know the form when you don't.

Once you get a reputation for being even a slightly dangerous shot, nobody will ever invite you again, or even include you in a team of paying Guns. It is a pretty certain way to end your game-shooting career.

Everyone does it

It would certainly be wrong to assume that the inexperienced or the young or indeed the very elderly are more likely to shoot dangerously. Far more frequently a very experienced gun, whose blood lust is up, will be the one who loses his sense of what is a safe shot or not. There isn't a shot in Britain who can say, hand on heart, that he has never fired a dangerous shot. As Max Hastings was brave enough to write in *The Field*, 'Everyone fires a dangerous shot at least once a season'. Another top grouse shot says: 'It is so tempting to swing through the line, particularly if you've been sitting there waiting for a long time. You get excited, you "commit" to a bird.'

It is likely that you will learn more about safety in those stomach-churning moments which follow the firing of a dangerous shot than from all the advice you will be given by any shooting instructor or book.

Where are the pickers-up and flankers?

Always err on the side of caution and only shoot when you are 100 per cent sure it is safe. If you are at the end of the line, you are more likely to be in range of peppering

a flanker so if you can't be absolutely sure, just don't shoot any birds in that direction. Only shoot at birds where you can see sky all around them, and never shoot into woods or hedges – you never know who might be standing inside a wood, or behind a hedge.

The end of the line is one of the most difficult positions to shoot from safely. Paradoxically this is where youngsters often start. When you are more experienced and have more confidence, you will be able to increase the angles you shoot but to begin with, it is much better to have a few less birds in your personal bag.

If shooting grouse or partridge, which fly much lower to the ground than pheasant, always check where the pickers-up are, and keep checking throughout the drive, as they tend to move around. If you suspect that the beaters are in range use your own discretion and just don't take any shots out front, even if the horn has not yet been blown.

Grouse moor safety

Use safety sticks

A very experienced loader on the grouse moor says: 'I always make sure that butt sticks are in the correct position and if an inexperienced Gun is shooting, I set them forward a bit more of the other butts, for extra safety.'

53

Even renowned grouse shot the Duke of Northumberland is only too aware of how easy it is to make a mistake. 'I always take my own sticks. It's quite easy to get disorientated, especially on a windy day in October… I feel naked without them!'

The fact that one of Britain's best grouse shots never shoots grouse without safety sticks illustrates how essential they are for everyone's protection. Inexperienced grouse shots should ideally also have a loader to keep them right. Swinging through the line, that is to say forgetting to raise your gun and then re-mount once the bird has passed through the line, is the biggest danger of grouse shooting. The safety sticks are planted either side of you on top of the butt, in line with your neighbouring Guns, so you don't lose track of where your neighbours are and to prevent you from swinging the gun too far. When the birds are bearing down upon you, it is all too tempting to follow them and swing right through. If you are shooting from a round butt, it is all too easy to get disorientated in the heat of the moment as to where everyone else is. Forgetting to raise your gun when the bird passes through the line is the most common cause of shooting accidents.

The horn

It is important to listen out for the horn when you know that very soon the beaters will be in range. Sometimes if there is a strong wind and you are wearing ear defenders you might fail to hear it. Use common sense and cease to shoot forward immediately you think that a beater could be close. Skylines vary, and even though you may not actually see anyone, your shot could be dangerous. Once the horn has been sounded on a driven grouse shoot, you can no longer take birds in front of you but you can take them behind you. As soon as the horn has gone, don't rest your gun on the top of the butt any more, lift it skywards, so approaching beaters don't have to look down your barrels.

Cartridge safety

At the beginning of each drive, before you put the first two cartridges into your gun, always look down the barrels and check for blockages. Even a small amount of mud blocking the end of the barrel will cause it to split, severely injuring your hand, or worse. Fingers and thumb can so easily be blown off and there are several people I know to whom this has happened. The worst danger is to have a 20-bore cartridge accidentally stuck in the barrels of a 12-bore gun. It is actually a very easy mistake to make in the heat of the moment, because the smaller 20-bore cartridge drops down low into the barrels, so you could wrongly assume you have dropped it on the ground, and so pop in another, 12-bore, on top. This will result in the barrels splitting and you could lose a finger or worse.

This sort of accident is more likely to occur if members of the same family use different calibres of gun, especially if they are in the habit of loading for each other from their pockets. A good loader will always check his pockets for any cartridges left over from a previous day, before putting new ones in.

So do always check barrels and pockets before the start of every drive. Equally important, if you are using an old English gun, is that you use cartridges that are chambered to the correct size. It does neither you nor the gun any favours to use a 2¾-inch cartridge through an old English.

Closing guns correctly

When closing your gun, you should always bring the stock up to the barrels with the barrels pointing down, and NOT barrels-to-stock. The reason for this particular safety rule was etched on my mind when my gun accidentally went off in the 2008 season on the grouse moor, as my loader was closing it. My right foot was inches away and it gave us both a bit of a fright! Fortunately he was an experienced loader and had closed the gun stock-to-barrels with the barrels pointing down, so the peat floor of the butt absorbed all the shot. If he had brought the barrels up to the stock, any ricochet from the stone walls of the butt would certainly have hit us in the face. I was thankful too that the dog was sitting safely behind us, not in front. Similarly, spectators should always sit behind or to the side of the Gun, never in front.

If you see anyone shooting dangerously

It is really important you say something straight away if you see anyone shooting dangerously, recommends grouse moor owner Sir Anthony Milbank.

'Immediately, during the drive, not after, shout out: "That's a bloody dangerous shot" or whatever. Really shock him, catch him in the act. The keeper should also yell, and if the owner is around or the shoot organiser he should deal with the incident immediately, during the drive.'

The worst thing you can do if someone has told you that you fired a dangerous shot, is to deny it. They will not be making the accusation lightly. Chances are you will suspect that maybe one of your shots was rather risky; it is very rare for a Gun to have absolutely no clue that they have fired a dangerous shot, unless it was a ricochet or they are very inexperienced. (Incidentally, even a peppering from a ricochet must be treated exactly the same as a dangerous shot, i.e. you must take full responsibility for it.)

People's reactions to being accused of dangerous shooting vary enormously. Some behave like perfect gentlemen, others refuse to take any blame at all, which can lead to some nasty goings-on in court. It is always best to apologise immediately.

As I have said, accidents are much more likely to happen on a grouse moor because the birds fly low to the ground and swinging down the line is a very real danger. Although you do hear of pepperings happening on rough shoot days and walked-up days, they can also occur on woodcock days where you are snap-shooting in woodland. Potentially of course such an accident could be fatal although I have never heard of a fatality. What is entirely feasible, though, is the loss of an eye, or worse, brain damage. It is imperative that everyone out on a grouse moor wears plastic protective glasses. Some keepers (especially those who've been peppered!) don't allow beaters and flankers out unless they have a pair. Some larger estates just bulk-buy them for everyone, which is a sensible approach, although Guns should take responsibility for themselves and arrive properly equipped.

Should the unthinkable happen and you do pepper someone, you should offer to take the injured party to hospital, either in your car, or else call an ambulance. Remember to leave your gun with your host or a fellow Gun as you don't want to turn up at A&E with it slung over your shoulder. If your victim does not want you to take him to hospital, you must respect his wishes. You should certainly sleeve up your gun for the rest of the day, unless your host insists that you carry on. It would no doubt be better for your confidence if you did.

My father had a charming Spanish guest to shoot for many years, and as he entered his early nineties this legendary shot, renowned in all of Spain, started to become a bit dangerous. One year he shot my father not once but twice, in the same day. As he was having the pellets removed by the doctor with the guest standing remorsefully by, he remarked, 'We have been friends for a long time, but if you carry on like this, I shall be forced to shoot back!'

Very British humour

Whilst any injuries out shooting must of course be taken extremely seriously, there are a few incidents which may amuse you. An American team of Guns took a day on one of Yorkshire's largest grouse moors. One of the Guns' wives was sitting outside the butt neighbouring her husband's. He swung through the line and shot her up the backside. Naturally he got a real ticking-off from the moor's owner. 'Now look here, you really must be more careful', he admonished him. The American, deeply mortified, replied: 'Thank God it was only my wife!'

Perhaps you have heard the story of an Arab gentleman who unfortunately peppered a beater a few years ago. Full of remorse, he gave the beater the keys to his brand new top-of-the-range Range Rover saying: 'Take it, it is yours now.' A group of beaters soon swarmed around him yelling: 'Shoot me! Shoot me next!'

A keeper at Coverdale who was flanking got shot in his right buttock: of course he complained like hell. The Gun in question got out his wallet and started peeling out note upon note. 'By God,' says the keeper, 'you can have t'other cheek for same amount!' Finally there is the now famous story of the Gun who shouts out to his neighbour: 'Oi! You've just peppered my wife!' to which the neighbour replies: 'Do you want to have a go at mine?'

In all seriousness, accidents out shooting are not good news. People may joke about them, but every shooting incident gives both the sport and the people involved a very bad name. They can end up costing the shoot host a lot of money, too; in a recent court case the host was fined, not the person who fired the dangerous shot, as he was deemed responsible for the safety of everyone on the day.

'Antis'

Protesters can be a very real danger out shooting. There is a strict code of conduct to which every shooting person must adhere for safety's sake. You should make sure that you read the code on the British Association for Shooting and Conservation website (www.basc.org.uk) before you go shooting, and stick to it.

Shoot protection agencies offer some degree of security because they can spot problems before they get serious and communicate to each other with radios to move the shooting party on to a different part of the moor.

However, retaining the services of a shoot protection agency is expensive and not always necessary unless you are shooting on the Glorious Twelfth or near to that date. Ultimately the 'antis' want column inches in the newspapers and the media are only really interested in grouse shooting around that date or if someone famous is involved. Whatever you do always avoid confrontation and immediately sleeve up your gun.

Safety Dos and Don'ts

Check the barrels are clear at the start of each drive

Clear previous days' cartridges from your pockets

When closing the gun, bring the stock up to the barrels not the barrels up to the stock

Walk with a broken gun or put it away in the gun sleeve between drives

Unload if you climb over a fence or stile

Unload and break the gun if you hand it to someone

Only take the shot if you are 100 per cent sure it is safe

Take extra care at the end of the line

Check and keep checking for pickers-up

Any spectators or dogs should sit behind you, close in, not in front

Use your discretion when shooting in front

Never shoot into a hedge or wood

Make sure your neighbouring Guns know where you are if you are not in view

Always hold your gun either broken, barrels pointing to the ground, or else closed and pointing to the sky

Never swing through the line, however tempting

Slide the safety catch on every time you hand the gun to your loader

Shooting well

One of the best ways to be a safe shot is to become a good shot. Hand to eye co-ordination is what it's all about. Some say that if you can hit a tennis ball, you can shoot.

Shooting clays is often where the novice begins. Some people are lucky enough to be born with a very natural ability: they smash their very first clays and are hooked for life. However, shooting is a sport you can pick up at any age and if well taught, you can reach a good level relatively quickly. Once you have become a proficient clay shot, the next step to becoming a good game shot is plenty of shoot days to build up your confidence. With confidence, come consistency and proficiency. Anyone can have moments of brilliance out shooting, but it is the Gun who is consistent, drive by drive, day by day, be it at grouse, duck or pheasant, who earns the right to be known as a good shot.

Mike Yardley, former British side-by-side champion, is the author of the BASC guide to shooting game, *Positive Shooting*. He has developed a new method of teaching.

> 'Natural Shooting places a new emphasis on sustained visual contact, co-ordinated body movement and the elimination of mental clutter. It recognises the importance of good footwork and the need to achieve a balanced, tension-free position at the moment the trigger is pulled. Combined with improved focus discipline, good body movement and a developed sense of timing, it unlocks awesome hand-eye co-ordination.

One of Mike's key pieces of advice to anyone wishing to improve their shooting is: 'You must stare the bird to death!'

Which gun to buy?

More often than not, the novice is taught to shoot with an over-and-under. This type of gun tends to be the shooting instructor's gun of choice because it is easier to shoot with, which gives great confidence to a beginner.

You may have picked up on the fact that some snobbery exists towards over-and-unders, especially by users of side-by-sides, which are traditionally known as 'gentleman's guns'. This can be confusing to the newcomer, who is keen to fit in and to do 'the right thing'. I myself have shot with both types but now shoot only with an over-and-under. Occasionally I hear snide comments, as a certain stigma seems to be associated with them. Perhaps this is because people regard over-and-unders as a more modern invention, or because they associate them with the world of competitive clay shooting – a branch of the sport rather looked down on by some of the game shooting fraternity.

Some history then, to enlighten or perhaps confuse you further: over-and-unders were actually developed at the same time as side-by-sides when percussion guns were first invented. However they were not as popular because people didn't believe the actions would hold together – they thought they would break. These guns were also much heavier because they needed more metal in the barrels and in the breech. Over time, the opinion of the majority won through and the side-by-side became the gun of choice.

When Boss & Co patented its famous over-and-under shotgun in 1909, the design changed forever. It was a strong shotgun, but also slim, light and graceful and utilised the reliable single trigger. This design has never been surpassed: perfecting the single trigger was probably the last development of importance with regard to sporting guns. Graham Halsey, managing director and owner of Boss & Co Ltd says:

'All the world clay-shooting champions, from skeet to trap, use over-and-unders. The Olympic team all use them: so it's to do with aiming and shooting consistently. But I think you should use whatever you shoot best with. If you've shot for twenty years with a side-by-side, why change?'

In 1914 Woodward, which was later bought by Purdey, followed suit and made its first over-and-under shot gun. Nigel Beaumont, chairman of Purdey, says:

'The over-and-under will throw its pattern higher than a side-by-side. The shot pattern generally prints sixty/forty high. So sixty per cent of the pattern is higher than the point of aim. Side-by-sides produce "flatter" shooting patterns with fifty per cent above and fifty per cent below the point of aim. With an over-and-under, the point of aim is not obscured by the horizontal barrels. It is a combination of these factors that renders the over-and-under, in my opinion, a superior shooting gun. Shooting people generally change from side-by-sides to over-and-unders. Seldom, indeed very seldom, have I seen people go the other way. But people still want side-by-sides, we make around sixty to forty side-by-sides to over-and-unders.'

Which bore?

The next big decision is whether to buy a 12-bore, 16-bore or 20-bore. There can be quite a difference in the killing range: some say that what you kill dead with a 12-bore you may only wound with a 20-bore, and what you may wound with a 12-bore, you may miss entirely with a 20-bore. But a lot depends on the cartridge and the choke of the gun, not to mention who's behind it.

It is quite unusual to see a 16-bore on the shooting field in the UK, but with a one-ounce cartridge they are meant to be the best all-round game gun. They are far more popular on the Continent.

In the UK, the popular choices are the 12-bore or the 20-bore. It is generally accepted that you have to be a much more accurate shot to shoot with a 20-bore but they are often chosen by ladies or youngsters as they are far lighter and easier to handle than a 12-bore.

Increasingly though, good male shots are opting to move down to a 20-bore. They prefer the reduced recoil, and find the lightness less tiring, especially if shooting six days out of seven.

Whichever gun you finally decide on, it goes without saying that you should take your time to make your choice, even up to a year, and get the best advice you can. Always try a gun out at a clay shooting ground before committing yourself.

The paperwork

If you haven't already got one, now is the time to start the process of applying for a shotgun certificate. This can be a lengthy business and you cannot buy a gun without one. You need two referees with professional status such as a doctor, a lawyer, a vicar or a bank manager. You need two passport photographs, which have to be certified to confirm that it really is you in the picture. Then a firearms officer will visit you at home and ask you all sorts of questions, some of which are quite personal. Your gun safe will also be inspected. It is worth bearing in mind that if you are the only shotgun licence-holder in your household, then only you should know where the keys to the safe are kept.

To shoot anywhere other than at a shooting school you also need to be fully insured so you should join either the BASC (British Association of Shooting and Conservation) or the Countryside Alliance. Both are excellent organisations and a lot of people are members of both.

The right fit

Having gained some shooting experience and bought your gun, take it straight to a gun fitter. Don't think for a moment you can get away with not bothering, because correct fitting is vital to your shooting long term. Try to find a professional with lots of experience to take the measurements and make the necessary adjustments.

You may need to be fitted for a gun more than once in your shooting career because the gun that fitted you when you were twenty-one might not necessarily fit you in your sixties, especially if you have put on weight. Everyone will mount the gun in a different way so it is hugely important to have your gun fitted to you. A gun should be like an extension of your arm and this can only be achieved through a professional fitting process.

The right fit?

At a shooting school you will be asked to use a Try-Gun and to aim at a pattern plate. Then measurements are taken and your new gun is taken away for the stock to be shortened, or lengthened, or the shape adjusted so that it is exactly right for you.

Choosing your cartridges

Having had your gun fitted, another important matter to consider is the type of cartridge that you will use.

All top shots tend to have a favourite cartridge. You will rarely see one turn up with a mixed bag of oddly assorted cartridges. You certainly don't want to be a cartridge bore, but it does help to get this part right. Once you find a brand of cartridge you like, try to stick with it and your choice will serve you well. Shot size and grams vary and so it is a very individual matter but also depends, of course, on whether you are shooting grouse or high pheasant. The rule of thumb is: the higher the bird, the smaller the shot size. For high pheasant a good choice would be a 5 shot, 30 or 32 gram, and on August grouse or partridge a 7 shot, 28 gram would be fine for a 12-bore.

If you are one of the rare people to shoot with a 16-bore, you must absolutely not run the risk of running out of cartridges! You are extremely unlikely to find anyone else in the line who can help you out. Another thing to remember about cartridges is that if you shoot with a 20-bore, do choose the correct gram. My ballistically-aware friends tell me that the kick of a 28 gram cartridge in a 20-bore is actually far greater than a 28 gram in a 12-bore, which defeats the usual point of shooting with a 20-bore in the first place, i.e. to reduce the amount of recoil. Many people agree that using a 30 gram cartridge in a 20-bore is to miss the point.

The ultimate goal of course is to shoot like a god with a 4.10. Not many people can achieve this, but it is impressive to watch.

Eyesight

At your very first shooting lesson the key thing is to determine which is your master eye. This is the only time in your whole shooting career when you point your (empty) gun at someone's head. This is so that the instructor can assess which is your dominant, or master, eye. On the whole a novice shot will be told to keep both eyes open but this is not suitable advice for everyone, as if you are 'cross-dominant' you are usually advised to close the eye opposite the sighting rib of the gun or even in some cases to change the shoulder you shoot from. Interestingly, nine out of ten women have 'indeterminate' eye dominance which means that both eyes fight for control when the woman takes aim.

Master eyes can mysteriously change with age, so it is worth having a check every ten or so years. Also, failing eyesight can obviously have a big impact on your shooting, so have regular check-ups, especially when you reach your sixties and seventies!

A loader at a famous ducal shoot in Leicestershire was getting frustrated with an American gentleman who was shooting like a drain. After two successive days, all the Gun had to show for his efforts was five pheasants and more than 500 spent cartridges. On the last drive the loader, desperate to try and help him asked, 'When you look along the gun, how much of the barrel can you see? Now, swing along the pylons on the telegraph wire over there, and can you see the little bobbles on the line?' The American gent apparently replied: 'What little bobbles?'

Once you have established that your eyesight is fine, know which is your master eye and have had your gun fitted, you will be off to the best start. After a series of regular clay shooting lessons, you will be well on the road to laying the foundations for being a good shot. Apart from practising on clays, a huge amount of experience at the real thing is all that lies between you and the best shots.

You don't have to be super-fit

Physical fitness is not of paramount importance, and you will often see very corpulent, twenty-stone individuals performing balletically and brilliantly. Never assume that the massively overweight Gun who can hardly get in and out of his vehicle without a crane won't be a fabulous shot! In fact shooting is an incredibly inclusive sport for those who are physically disabled or wheelchair-bound. I have seen one-armed Guns outperform their able-bodied neighbours in the line and, for the wheelchair-bound, it is perfectly possible to shoot from a sitting position. In fact my uncle, Sam Nickerson, was a fabulous shot despite for the last twenty years of his shooting career suffering from advancing multiple sclerosis. He used to shoot from a converted armchair which his loader stood behind, turning him towards whichever direction the birds were coming from.

William Sporborg, bloodstock investor and former point-to-point jockey, says:

'I was the second worst shot in England. In fact on one day's shooting the bag was over two hundred and I didn't register a single bird. I was a very, very bad shot... Then, when I broke my back and couldn't go golfing, hunting or racing any more, I decided to concentrate on shooting and I was very lucky that so many people invited me. I had no knowledge, I very much started from scratch. I now shoot around fifteen to eighteen days a season. I travel all over the country. Once you are sitting on your peg, if you are disabled you have as good a chance as the next man. Wheelchairs and wheelchair-users are normally a pain for everyone to have around, but in my specially converted quad bike I can be quite helpful out shooting and if a goose or something is shot, they can fling it on the back.'

The will to kill

There is one vital element without which you will never quite make it as a top game shot. Put simply, you must have a very strong desire to bring the bird down. You must harbour in you the instinctive will to kill. Some shots have this in spades, which means that sometimes they are labelled aggressive, or just plain greedy, but it is their killer instinct coming to the fore. A shot who is over-polite and always concerned about whose bird is whose, might be relaxing to shoot next to, but he won't ever be the greatest shot. You need the blood lust to be brilliant.

Don't think, though, that you need to be a countryman brought up killing rabbits and birds from the cradle to have your share of blood lust. City types, more used to fighting it out in the concrete jungle, slip very easily and quickly into this new role and have a real hunger for the kill. Perhaps that is why shooting is enjoying such a renaissance as the sport of choice for corporate entertainment. As long as this killer instinct is harnessed in a positive way, it is what will make the newcomer to shooting shine on the shooting field.

Practice makes perfect

Between seasons, clay shooting is a good way of keeping your eye in. Some Guns turn their noses up at clay practice, others regularly shoot at their local shooting ground all year round and some just turn up for a couple of pre-season sharpeners. A course of pre-season lessons with an instructor is vital for enabling the less experienced Gun to improve his familiarity with the different game birds. Always ensure that your instructor knows that you are there to practise for game bird shooting. If you are going to be shooting predominantly pheasant, there is not much point in spending too long on low, going-away birds, although all types will help your shooting because practice will speed up your reactions, improve your footwork and help you to mount the gun consistently.

In fact I highly recommend a few clay sessions outside the shooting season for everyone, experienced shot or novice. Keeping your eye in and your reactions fast will improve your enjoyment enormously.

Having an off day

Everyone has an off day sooner or later. Even some of the best shots find they have a drive where they just cannot connect at all. It is bound to happen at some stage, and for the beginner it might happen more often than not. It is just one of those things, and how you react to having a bad day is crucial, because, funnily enough, you will be judged on this more than on any lack of shooting prowess.

Sometimes, the birds will simply get the better of you because they are more difficult. Peter Schwerdt, a fanatical shot who shoots over 100 days a year and as a rule is deadly accurate, emphasises this:

'Form is a fickle mistress, she can visit you and she can leave you. Everyone who shoots really well has a time when they shoot badly. You can be brilliant one day, and terrible the next – it's all in your head. You have to clear the clutter from your head. And then, there will always just be those days when the birds are more difficult...'

Keep smiling

It's not just being off form which could cause you to have a bad day: there can be lots of reasons. You might have fired twenty-odd cartridges for one bird and then not be able to find it. Or due to sheer bad luck birds may 'split' on you, flying to your neighbour on each side, but not coming to you. Or your ejector might fail, causing you to have to prise out the cartridges yourself, making loading so slow and tortuous that you fluff the chances you do get. Any of these scenarios are guaranteed to make your blood boil. The tricky part is to keep calm and stay the happy, charming, 'perfect guest' you need to be, in order to be invited again!

The most important thing to remember is always to smile and make favourable comments about the birds after every drive, regardless of how few cartridges you have fired or how badly you have shot. Inside you might be fuming, but try to keep

It is better to have too many cartridges than too few

all your emotions in check, especially if your host is nearby! Resist at all costs the urge to grumble – good sportsmanship is what it's all about. It is worth remembering that nobody else cares if you are missing birds, as long as *they* are not.

Never blame others for your own lack of skill. One shoot host recalls a let-day guest who was shooting so badly that in his frustration he started tearing a strip off his loader, criticising him, and then started having a go at the keeper. He was told in no uncertain terms to seek pastures new next season.

Take sufficient cartridges

If you are going to leave your cartridge bag in the vehicle for a drive, make sure you pocket enough cartridges, just in case. It is always better to have too many than too few. Ask if you are unsure about how many drives will take place before you will be returning to the vehicles so you know whether or not to take your cartridge bag.

Keep schtum

As with any sport, keep positive, and try to look ahead to the next drive with confidence. If anyone asks you directly how you got on in a particularly difficult drive where you shot nothing, just say something like, 'They flew so well! I'm afraid I didn't do them justice'; or 'They were too good for me!'.

If you had a blank drive (one where you didn't even fire a shot) don't mention it, keep schtum. Don't tell the host, even if he asks you a direct question about how the drive went. Just mutter something along the lines of 'I missed some good chances', or 'I mucked up the drive, don't have anything to show for it I'm afraid', and hope to do better in the next drive. Whatever you do, if you are missing a lot don't resort to shooting low birds if you can't shoot the high ones. It's considered very bad form to shoot a low bird and doing so will not enhance your reputation. In general, keep positive, keep cheerful and keep trying!

Shooting Well – Dos and Don'ts

Get your gun properly fitted and confirm your master eye

Practise on lots of clays before venturing out on to the shooting field

Take a loader/instructor with you on your first few forays

Keep focused, keep a clear head

Check your footwork

Mount your gun and pull the trigger in one smooth movement

Don't 'poke' at the birds, keep your gun moving

Keep up a cheerful front and stay positive

Don't complain, sulk or blame anyone else for your poor form

Remember, it could be worse, you could still be in the office

---

5
Manners on the Field

'Shooting courteously is vital but almost a misnomer because the very act of shooting is, by its nature, aggressive'
Jonathan Kennedy

After safety, shooting courteously is one of the most important attributes of the perfect guest. Nothing upsets and spoils the day more if your neighbours have been helping themselves to your birds. If you have ever been on the receiving end of this sort of behaviour, you will know that having your birds consistently poached is no laughing matter.

How do you know if the bird is yours?

Giles Catchpole, writing in his very comprehensive book about shooting, *Birds, Boots and Barrels*, published by Quiller, gives a great description of how you can tell if a bird is yours or not:

> 'If you imagine a solid wall bisecting the gap between you and each of your neighbours, the channel between the two walls is your polite area of activity. Your safe arcs of fire may be greater, indeed, should be greater, but this is where politeness dictates you participate. Only depart from it if your neighbour is unloaded and you have nothing else in your airspace, or to address a wounded bird.'

The ins and outs of poaching

A good rule of thumb is: always let a few birds fly on to your neighbour unscathed, especially if he happens to be your host!

Some of Britain's best shots are also the most polite people to be drawn beside. Being caught in a 'Percy sandwich', that is to say pegged between the Duke of Northumberland and his brother, Lord James Percy, is a position most Guns would regard with the utmost awe, and not a little horror. But the truth of the matter is that neither will pile into their neighbours' birds, they just focus on their own. They are polite to neighbouring Guns but of course deadly to the birds in their own airspace. As James Percy says:

> 'Never be greedy, as this is the worst fault after being dangerous. If in doubt, leave a bird to your neighbour. There is nothing worse than someone constantly letting fly at his and his neighbours' birds.'

Ralph Northumberland agrees:

> 'Don't land birds in your host's butt or wipe his eye too often. Also, tell him how beautifully he shot that drive.'

Jonathan Kennedy says:

> 'If you are in any doubt about whether a bird is yours or your neighbour's, err on the side of caution and be generous. It is an essential courtesy and part of the unspoken code.'

Jonathan continues:

> 'Shooting courteously is vital, but almost a misnomer because the very act of shooting is by its nature, aggressive, and harks back to a bygone era when prey was to be hunted and your wits were pitted against a wild quarry... Occasionally you might make a mistake and take a bird nearer your neighbour. If it happens, which it is bound to occasionally, immediately apologise and acknowledge the act, calling out "Sorry!", even if it's a marginal situation. Competitiveness has no place on the shooting field.'

If you behave in a cavalier fashion, and keep on pinching your neighbours' birds, you run the risk of beginning a mini 'war' with that neighbouring Gun and he might spend the rest of the day getting his revenge on you. Unless you are a top shot, it's not worth the risk and besides, this is not what shooting is about.

These battles usually only occur out pheasant or partridge shooting. Willie Peel says: 'There are two rules: grouse, where it is total warfare, open to everybody and anything is fair, and pheasant, where a greater degree of discretion is preferable.'

If you are a crack shot – be considerate

There will be times out grouse shooting when the prevailing wind will mean that all the birds will fly in a similar direction and your neighbour might not get the chance at any unless they have first flown past you. This is not usually a problem because you are likely

Don't brag, try to be modest

to miss at least some. But if you happen to shoot like a god, then be considerate and allow a few birds to fly on so that your neighbour can get his gun off occasionally too.

I heard a story about one guest, a fabulous shot, much prized for end of season grouse-culling, who was pegged next to his host, on his right, on a grouse moor. The birds were all coming from the right, heading straight for them but at an angle which meant the host could only take them behind the line. Unfortunately for the host, his guest shot dead each and every bird as it flew towards them. Each one followed exactly the same flight path. By the end of the drive, there were seven birds, about a foot apart, scattered all around in front of the host's butt. This did not go down at all well! The last thing you want as the perfect guest is to gain the reputation of being greedy: to be a good and considerate shot should be your aim.

When you are under attack from 'poachers'

Most people behave incredibly well out shooting, but sometimes good manners do fly out of the window, which can spoil the day for everyone. Not all the Guns you draw next to will be particularly polite and you must also be ready for the different customs of different nationalities. The Spanish in particular do not have the same regard for poaching etiquette as we do in Britain and you may find yourself under serious attack from a neighbour! If ever you are in this situation, an old trick learned from my father is simply to wait until there is nothing flying over you, and then to fire your gun up into the sky, at nothing. Afterwards, your neighbour will more than likely approach you and ask you what you were shooting at. To which you reply:'I was just letting you know that I had a gun too'.

Other ruses to get back at your neighbour (as outlined by Ralph Northumberland in a Barbour leaflet called Hot Tips For Hot Shots) are:

'Open your gun every time he shoots a bird and looks round to see who's watching, to create doubt in the offender's mind as to whether he or you shot the bird.

Shout "Yours!" very loudly every time he's about to fire.

Count his spent cartridges after each drive and gently shake your head.'

Another tactic you can use out grouse shooting if you feel a Gun has had more than his fair share of birds is to do what some friends did. They waited until the greedy Gun was in his butt, ready for the next drive, and then casually strolled over; one distracted him while the other fixed the pages from a broadsheet newspaper to the front of his butt. Naturally all the birds in that drive split on him!

Most probably, though, you will be more concerned about poaching someone else's birds by mistake than about yours being taken, especially if you are a novice shot or aspire to be the perfect guest.

Poaching on purpose

Of course I am not saying that you can never poach from a friend, in fact it can be rather amusing and wakes them up a bit! But you should only do this to a very good friend, and then only occasionally. I know some people who set out with a purpose, to poach from their neighbouring Guns all day. You see them piling into every bird that flies anywhere near them, or their neighbour, or even one up from their neighbour. In my view this is not particularly 'sporting' in the proper sense of the word as it is not fair to the birds, which might have as many as six or eight rounds of lead fired at them, instead of two or four. Every bird should be given a fair and sporting chance – and bear in mind that mouthfuls of lead don't make good eating. If you get in the habit of doing this amongst friends and then shoot elsewhere, you may forget your manners and start piling into other people's birds out of habit. It can also be dangerous, as everyone gets more and more competitive and carried away. If your neighbouring Guns are not as adept as you are, it will definitely spoil their day. It is certainly not a great way to behave if you want to be asked again.

Back-Guns

I was shooting up in Aberdeenshire a few years ago and a friend was standing as back-Gun behind me. I was getting into the swing of it, when suddenly I realised that the back-Gun wasn't waiting for me to fire the second shot before piling into the birds. Then he even started shooting at them way in front, before I'd even mounted my gun! Needless to say, when you are a back-Gun, you should wait until the Gun in front has had their chance, and let off two shots, before you fire yourself. Conversely, if you know there is a back-Gun behind you, be considerate and leave him the odd bird.

Jonathan Young was once pegged as back-Gun behind a really good shot.

'The etiquette here is tricky. If I were behind my close friends it would be a point of honour for them not to let a single bird through – and I would take the joke! But this chap was an acquaintance – and hell, could he shoot. No bird survived his gauntlet of fire until, at the end, he let through one bedraggled cock, about ten yards high. I also let the bird pass and at the end of the drive thanked him for giving me this one opportunity of a shot.

The Gun concerned went into full spluttering mode and told me that's what I could expect if I insisted on using an over-and-under!'

Back-Gun?

71

Nothing at close range

Similarly, try not to 'pillowcase' birds, that is to say, shoot them too close in, so that the sky fills with feathers and the shot rips the bird apart. These can't be sold off later to a game dealer and it is not sporting. A loader I knew always used to remark 'Plucked' whenever his Gun shot one too close in. One Gun apologised to a picker-up about the state of a bird he'd 'pillowcased' and the picker-up replied: 'Pillowcased?! More like you've made pâté out of it!'

A friend told me a story of a fellow Gun, known to some as Buster, normally a very good shot, who once took a bird almost on the end of his barrels. His neighbour went to find it in the game wagon and hid the bird until lunchtime. As the lunch lady served up plates of delicious roast beef, Buster waited expectantly for his plate, but on it appeared his bird from the second drive, complete with guts hanging out and feathers everywhere…

Obey your shoot host

Being a courteous shot can also manifest itself by you listening out for and remembering any instructions from your host. If you have been told not to shoot woodcock or to leave the white 'marker' pheasants, then to do otherwise would be seen as very rude. Often there is a fine involved, which goes to a good shooting cause.

A friend of mine who's a bit of a prankster tells me about a trick he once played on someone out shooting.

'We were all warned of a fine for the white pheasant. The drive was in a ride and I was able to sneak behind the Guns up the line, unseen in the trees, where I deliberately shot the white pheasant behind one of them. When he refused to take responsibility for the shot, even though the bird had landed right behind him, I offered to pay his fine, which made him even more cross. Then while he was discussing it with the keeper I popped the bird into a small zipped up bag in his vehicle and went home thinking no more of it. Months

Pillowcasing

later I was in the Caribbean, at a drinks party, where I slide into a group who appear to be having a fascinating discussion with a lot of "oohs" and "aahs". The general consensus was that somebody had committed a heinous act and should be shot. I caught snippets about a "terrible smell" so the staff (he had a large imposing house) got in Dynorod…no change so they thought it could be a dead rat under the floor so the floorboards came up …then the smell was traced to some wood panelling, that too came down… until eventually someone found the zipped bag hanging in the boiler room where he kept his cap, cashmere gloves, ear defenders and so on, and it had a stinking green goo dripping out of it! After that, whenever I knew we were likely to see each other at a party I would make my excuses and keep well away!'

Someone told me another story about a Gun who, sick of having his grouse poached all day, decided to take his revenge. When the offender was having tea, he went to his car and got a flounder (he was also a keen fisherman) and put it under the greedy Gun's bonnet, above the engine. The journey down from Scotland was rather a smelly one!

'Good shot, Sir!'

Noticing your neighbour's good shots

A 'right and left' is when you shoot one bird, then another, without lowering the gun from your shoulder. (If you lower the gun between shots, it apparently doesn't count, but that's for purists!) It is always a thrill when you manage to do this, and if you see your neighbour do so, it would be polite to congratulate him. Always hold fire until your neigh-bouring Gun has shot both barrels at birds coming towards you from him. If you see your neighbour shoot a really high bird, it's perfectly acceptable to shout out during the drive a big cry of 'Good shot' or 'Well done!' These little acts of courtesy are much appreciated out shooting and imagine how pleased you would feel if someone noticed your best shots.

73

'Frightful bad luck, old boy…'

Eye-wiping

'Wiping someone's eye' refers to shooting and killing a bird which someone else has missed. Where the saying comes from is unclear, but I have heard it said that if you manage to shoot a bird your neighbour has missed, it is the cause for such hilarity that it makes you cry with laughter! Certainly eye-wiping is often a cause for celebration for the person who manages to do it, particularly if the one who missed is known to be a good shot. However, there are some dos and don'ts: always make sure your neighbour has fired both barrels before you have a go, and don't do it too often. That would be making it painfully obvious that your neighbour shoots like a drain. Of course you must shoot if the bird is wounded and needs finishing off.

Some shots believe that if the bird has managed to fly past unscathed having had two shots fired at it, then it deserves to continue on in peace. John Plumptre, who lives and breathes shooting, believes it is poor form to consistently wipe your neighbour's eye. 'When I was a youngster I remember a man doing this to me and it made me feel so small, I vowed I would never do it.' Even John admits to a bit of eye-wiping occasionally, 'but usually only on a grouse moor in a big year'.

On the subject of youngsters shooting, it is a good idea to be generous. There is just no merit in being a greedy shot when you have a youngster pegged next to you. As James Percy says: 'Always make sure a youngster gets a chance to wipe your eye. Or tell him or her how well they have done. It's a dog eat dog world and a little encouragement goes a long way.'

Low birds

Naturally low birds should be ignored in favour of higher birds, especially if you suspect that there is a specific bag your host is aiming for. If you are a bit of a dead-eye dick and rarely miss, you don't really want to be accused of personally shooting the bag by lunchtime.

Just go carefully and stick to the more challenging birds. However if all the birds are fairly low, holding back too much can look as if you are being too picky a shot. You have to gauge it right. You wouldn't refuse food at a dinner party because it wasn't exactly to your liking, would you? You will just know not to accept an invitation to that shoot another time. So choose the more challenging birds whenever possible and have the occasional shot at ones you wouldn't normally attempt if there aren't any others available.

In the same way that shooting low birds should be discouraged, you shouldn't take wild shots at birds out of range, because this would only result in them being pricked, and very hard to pick. Shoot only what is in a good killable range of your gun.

No slamming doors or dawdling

As good guests, you must also try to move off swiftly to your peg, without too much slamming of vehicle doors or dawdling to chat to the other Guns, which will slow the drive down. Always bear in mind that there are about thirty to forty people waiting for you to get into position. Save the chatting for after the drive. If a fellow Gun is elderly or infirm, you could offer to swop places with him to save him a gruelling walk, but this suggestion could sometimes be met with indignant fury! Again, you have to judge the specific situation.

Shoot staff

Apart from courtesy towards your fellow Guns, you must always try to be courteous to all the shoot staff. They are very much part of the day. There is nothing more off-putting than seeing Guns behave in a patronising or offhand manner to shoot staff. Word will get back faster than you might think to your host, who will take a dim view. Regardless of whether you are paying for the day or not, you won't be invited back. Shoot staff are there to make your day enjoyable, so show appreciation for their efforts whenever you can.

On the whole, the men and women who act as beaters or flankers and pickers-up do so for the love of the sport and the joy of being out in the country. They are quite possibly keen shooting people themselves, and by taking part in a local shoot, if they are reliable and frequent helpers, they stand a good chance of being invited to the end of season Keeper's Day. I am sure they all appreciate the pay packet at the end of the day too, but this is not a job they do purely for the money. Nine times out of ten they love the countryside and enjoy being part of the team. Just in case you are unsure of all the different jobs on a shoot day, there follows a brief description.

Stops and flankers

You don't really get flankers on a pheasant shoot; they are called stops. At the start of the day their job is to stand in a particular spot for a couple of hours to ensure the birds 'hold' in a wood or covert. It is often a thankless task and they are the unsung heroes of the day. There are usually around three or four out on a shoot and they appear in a line at the bottom of the game crop or wood, standing still and just quietly tapping a stick throughout the drive, to stop the pheasants running out of the coverts instead of taking flight.

On partridge and grouse shoots, a flanker's job is vital. They are there to turn the birds back if they look as if they will fly out to the sides, and adopt various tactics to achieve this. There could be up to twelve flankers on a grouse day, six each side of the beaters. They are often retired beaters who can no longer do a whole day's beating any more. Their great experience is invaluable, and some have it in spades. I have met flankers, some in their eighties, who adore coming out, and don't miss a single day all season. Sometimes their eyesight and hearing can be so poor that they don't notice a pack of grouse coming their way, and on one well-known moor, the head keeper blows a whistle to alert the flankers to flag: the system seems to work well!

Flankers and stops are an integral part of the day. By chatting to them, you can learn all sorts of things about the estate, the area, and any amount of local gossip. Flanker and cartridge-picker-upper Andrew Horn is a regular on the grouse moors near Richmond. A retired railwayman, he loves coming out and is very fit and sprightly.

'I've hardly missed a day on the moors, I've been out six days out of seven every day since 12 August. I will keep going until I drop. This is my fifth year of coming out. I'm retired, I come from the south but I've come back to my roots now. I love the exercise and if it's a nice day I'd be going for a walk anyway, so to be paid £40 is very welcome!'

Peter Schollar is seventy-five years old and a very experienced flanker. Being a good flanker is not easy, he explained to me.

'It all depends on how the wind blows, you have to keep well down in the heather sometimes, and then others, stay visible. I'm usually the second one in. I've been coming here fourteen years. I also pick up the birds from the butts and take them down to the game cart.'

Beaters

A beater's job on a pheasant shoot is very different to that of a grouse beater, where they are sometimes known as 'drivers'. The distance covered on a pheasant shoot is far less; usually the beaters have to walk through a wood or game crop, spaced out in as straight a line as possible. They tap their sticks on trees and thrash the under-growth as they walk, which can be hard work if there are a lot of brambles and fallen trees. Keeping a straight line sounds easier than it is in practice.

On a grouse moor, each drive can involve a two- to three-mile march, through knee-high heather and boggy patches. Whilst waiting for the signal to start marching, beaters have to sit in the heather in their positions in all weathers, usually too far from the next beater for any cosy chatting. Once it's time to start, it is no joke: keeping up, keeping in a straight line, striding along and waving your flag while trying to avoid falling into hidden holes or ditches covered by heather is not for the faint-hearted. So when the beaters stream past your butt, don't just ignore them. Try to catch their eye and thank them, or tell them what a great drive you had. Naturally they really appreciate it when their efforts are recognised.

Don't ignore the beaters

In August, beaters often tend to be schoolchildren, or university students. But in term-time, grouse moors are dependent on teams of dedicated beaters who regularly beat for the same estate.

Mary Wearmouth, in her sixties, is a regular beater on Reeth, near Richmond in Yorkshire, who has earned the right to command her own section of the line. This involves carrying an estate radio to stay in contact with the keepers and it is her job to keep 'her' beaters under control and walking in a straight line…

'My grandfather was a keeper and when I was child I was desperate to go beating but I couldn't because they didn't allow girls. My brother was four years younger and he was allowed to go. I first went out beating in 1985 and now I'm retired I never miss a day. What I love most is the teamwork, and being out on the moor.'

Although beaters always used to be men or boys, it is quite usual these days to see women out beating, and many of them use this as a way of keeping fit, rather than going to the gym!

Help your neighbour

Aside from being kind and courteous to all the shoot staff you meet, you can also show good manners after the drive is over by helping your neighbouring guns pick up their birds. If you are all picked, and they appear to be still missing some birds, you could go over and help out, even if you have no dog. Just striding off isn't very friendly, and the chances are that you may have seen where one of his birds fell.

Handling dead birds

Sometimes you can help by bringing any birds from your peg to the game cart, unless you are specifically told to leave the game on your peg. Just a quick word about handling dead birds – don't ever just chuck them in a pile. The meat bruises easily, and also it shows respect to your quarry and to your host if you lay the birds out neatly in a row at your peg. Most likely they will be heading to a game dealer which will be a source of revenue for your host.

Leaving the shoot early

If you have been invited to shoot, it is simply not acceptable to leave before the last drive. People who assume that they can do this have no appreciation for the effort that goes into a day's shooting. Unless there really is a valid reason not to do so, then you should see the last drive through to the end. I was grouse shooting on a friend's family moor about fifteen years ago with a chap who insisted he had to leave the last drive early. When I asked him what was so pressing, his reply was that he had a flight to catch as he had a business meeting in Germany on the Monday. (It was Saturday.) Naturally I then asked why he didn't fly out on the Sunday instead, and he told me that the airline ticket was far cheaper if you took in a Saturday night! When you consider the expense of putting on a grouse day, that was a pretty shocking response.

Leaving straight from the shooting field after the last drive is acceptable if you have to drive a very long distance, so long as you have tipped the keeper and said your goodbyes to your fellow Guns, of course.

In a nutshell

Everyone involved in shooting must act as good ambassadors for the sport. Remember that the day is not just about you; everybody has equal rights to enjoyment.

Good Manners – Dos and Don'ts

Never poach, unless you know the person well

Abide by the rules of the day regarding what you may or may not shoot

Don't slam vehicle doors or dawdle on your way to your peg

Don't be greedy, be aware of your neighbours

Don't raise your gun to easy, low-flying targets

Be the first to apologise after the drive if you did take a bird from your neighbour

Encourage others and praise their good shots

Never mock someone for shooting badly

Never brag about how well you are shooting

Don't take wild out-of-range shots

Offer to swop places with elderly or unfit fellow guns to save them from having to hike up a steep hill, or across tricky ground

Never fire late shots at departing grouse – you'll probably only prick them

Treat all shoot staff with courtesy and amiability and remember to thank everyone

---

6
Marking Your Birds and Picking Up

'To be honest, Guns with out of control dogs are a nuisance'
John Holloway, picker-up

Working your gundog after the drive can be one of the most enjoyable aspects of shooting. Many Guns have never experienced this themselves but can derive a lot of pleasure from watching the pickers-up. It is wonderful to see the dogs 'hoover' an area to find that elusive bird you had thought was lost. As a Gun, there is nothing more satisfying than seeing all your birds accounted for and lying on your peg.

Pick your birds

One thing is certain: the aim of every Gun should be to attempt to find his birds after a drive, dog or no dog. However, you frequently see people sleeve up their guns at the end of a drive and just stand around chatting, or they walk off, without making any attempt to retrieve their birds or have a word with the pickers-up.

A lot of people can shoot well enough for everyone to think they are 'old hands' and know just what they are doing: yet at the end of the drive they let themselves down in this glaringly obvious way. Perhaps they assume that as they don't have a dog, they are somehow exempt from this activity. After the drive is over they even seem more interested in picking up their cartridges and working out their bird-to-cartridge ratio than in picking up their birds. Picking up cartridges is an excellent practice, but preferably only after birds are picked.

Strolling past birds without picking them is the biggest gripe of shoot hosts and shoot staff and can give you a really bad name. After all it is not the job of the pickers-up to pick all the easy birds that land out in the open near your peg. Their job is to retrieve the trickier ones that have fallen some way off, or the wounded ones which may have run into thick undergrowth.

Talk to the pickers-up

If you know for a fact you wounded a bird, it is your responsibility to seek out a picker-up and inform him. The chances are he may have seen it, marked it, and even picked it already. But then again, he may have been busy and not seen it, so the onus is on you to make contact and find out.

Mark Firth of the Countryside Alliance says:

'Some Guns, rightly, get very hot under the collar about pickers-up picking "their" birds. At the earliest opportunity, the Gun should make contact with the pickers-up and let them know if he would like to pick some birds himself. It makes me so mad to see some Guns go through the whole day without speaking to a single picker-up or beater, especially on a grouse moor, when the beaters have walked perhaps three miles and the Gun just ignores them, as if they are not there. They also miss out on one of the key aspects – that everyone is involved.'

Chatting to the shoot staff, the pickers-up or keeper, can add hugely to your day's enjoyment: you start to get to know the characters involved and that adds a new dimension. They are there to help you, but you need to do your bit too and tell them roughly where your birds fell, and how many there were.

Don't specify unless certain

If you are not sure whether it's a cock or a hen bird which is missing, don't specify! I saw a novice shot recently tell a picker-up with great conviction: 'I got a cock bird which landed just over that hedge.' Two pickers-up then duly hunted around where the man had pointed for about ten minutes but still no cock bird was found – although a hen bird was retrieved from the exact spot almost immediately. Eventually the Gun had to admit rather sheepishly: 'Oh, well, maybe it was a hen bird then...' Even an experienced Gun can get it wrong, especially when the drive hots up.

A picker-up on picking up

John Holloway, from Sedgefield, retired from a career in dentistry, has spent thirty years trialling dogs in field trials up and down the country. In 2007–08 he went picking up on seventy-four days and in 2008–09 topped a hundred days. He has fourteen dogs, a mix of labradors, springer spaniels and cockers. He usually takes out five or six dogs at a time and picks up on both grouse days and pheasant days on three main estates in Yorkshire and County Durham.

He confirms that 'the biggest beef we pickers-up have is when the Gun shoots, then puts his gun in the sleeve and walks off. It would make our job much easier if we knew how many we'd got to find – it's all about communication'.

Sir Anthony Milbank, who owns a grouse moor and pheasant shoot in North Yorkshire, blames big corporate days for the current trend of picking-up apathy and general ignorance. He says:

'They have huge bags, nobody has a dog, and there are highly professional teams of pickers-up, usually one behind each Gun, so Guns are actually encouraged to walk off, without picking up, as they are usually being hurried on to the next drive. If you've been used to big corporate days, you imagine all shoots to be the same and it can be difficult to switch. People will tell you: "But I haven't a clue where they landed! I don't have a dog!" if asked why they are not actively seeking their birds.'

Wait for the whistle

Naturally all picking up is done only once the whistle has been blown. On the whole, pickers-up only allow their dogs to retrieve strong 'runners' during the drive, but never throughout the drive, in case their dogs start to pin down tired birds. Naturally Guns must not allow their dogs to start picking up until the end of the drive. As Mark Firth says:

'If a bird is wounded the primary consideration is putting it out of its misery. If it has landed behind the Guns, the pickers-up should send a dog for it there and then. But there is nothing worse than dead birds being picked up from around the Guns, especially if they have their own dogs with them.'

Be honest about what you shot

However bad a day you are having, don't ever invent birds that aren't there. Apparently one trick pickers-up use when they believe they've been sent off after a 'mythical' bird, is to have a bird in a pocket which can then suddenly be brandished triumphantly, to bring the whole episode to an end!

Mastering the art of marking your birds

The key to efficient picking up is marking the birds correctly. Marking birds is an art, which even some very experienced shots haven't mastered. Some grouse shots use those little marker boards with an erasable pen to help them keep count. But mostly (particularly when pheasant or partridge shooting) you just have to keep as close a count as possible in your head.

Marking YOUR birds

During the drive, to help your memory, you can repeat a little mantra (even though some people might think you are bit bonkers) as each bird falls, where it lands, so that by the end you can say with clear authority to any picker-up: 'I got two out front, one to the right, two behind and one wounded, far back near the hedge.' Natural markers, such as a tree or a fence post, may help you too. Word will soon get around if you can mark accurately, assuming all the birds are where you say they are! You may well find that on subsequent drives the pickers-up will come to you rather than to others, if they know they can trust your marking ability.

Of course if you have your own gundog, you can rely on him to have done a bit of marking for you! Certainly Guns with dogs pick up the correct number of birds much faster than those without…but whether they are the 'right' birds often remains in doubt…

Gundog etiquette

There is no denying that having a gundog sitting at your peg adds hugely to the day. Sending your dog for a tricky retrieve, and seeing him scent it, find it, and bring it to you, sends tingles down the spine. But by the same token, if your dog lets you down by running in during the drive, or worse still, flushing out the pheasants meant for the next drive, you will wish the ground had opened up and swallowed you. The choice is yours – if you want to be asked again, think twice about taking your dog if there is any chance of him misbehaving.

The naughty dog

We've all seen them, and laughed at them, but for the owner of a naughty dog, each shoot day is fraught with peril and embarrassment. Picture the scene: you arrive late, the Guns are assembled in front of the house, you open the boot of your vehicle and your over-excited labrador bounds out, jumps up at all the Guns, then deposits a huge steaming turd on your host's lawn. He strains on his slip-lead, tripping up anyone who gets in his way. Throughout the day he whines and howls loudly during every drive, manages to pull out the heavy duty corkscrew brought specially to restrain him, and proceeds to run wild throughout the drive, picking up, dropping, and gnawing on the birds he picks. At elevenses, he pees on a Gun's stockinged leg and then leaps up and manages to pull the basket of sausage rolls off the bonnet of the Land Rover and begins wolfing them down. Then he puts his muddy paws all over the host's wife's new suede jacket. Later, in hot pursuit of a rabbit, you see him go tearing across the game covert, emptying it of all the birds meant for the next drive…

Some Guns really don't give a damn how badly their dog behaves. I certainly don't suggest you follow the example of one particular guest, who, a few seasons ago, arrived on the morning of the shoot, got out of his car and greeted the assembled Guns. He opened the boot of his vehicle to let out his black lab and told him: 'Now, I'll meet you back here at 5pm, make sure you're on time or I'll leave without you!'

There is a saying that a polo pony can be ruined in seven minutes. Well, by the same token, a gundog can be ruined in hours. As the owner, you must be patient and put the time in and you will be rewarded. If you don't have time to train the dog yourself, then you need to invest many hundreds of pounds in sending it off for training. Once it is trained do not be frightened of sending your dog back for refresher courses. You should visit the trainer and spend time with him as he trains the dog, certainly a half day every fortnight.

Janet Menzies, writer and champion field-trialler, used to have an infamous cocker spaniel called Dutch, who was renowned up and down the country for emptying drives by charging through the game coverts. On doing this one day, and ruining the next drive, his charm failed to impress the keeper. Janet says:

> 'The keeper was purple with rage, he really was furious with me. I replied: "I don't know why you are making such a fuss, he's emptied far better drives than this!" At which point the keeper was so rude to me that my husband took offence and gave his tip to the Game Keepers' Benevolent Fund.'

Occasionally, though, Janet found that Dutch was actually in demand, purely for his propensity to empty drives.

> 'One day I was shooting at a well-known Exmoor shoot. The host came up to me after one of the drives and said: "I think you should work Dutch." I replied, "No, I'm keeping him in the car." But my host insisted – "I think you should

'Your dog's picked up some bad habits this summer.'

work Dutch", he repeated. At last I understood: we were shooting far too many birds and he wanted a few less in the next drive!'

Janet's golden rules for gundogs on the field are: 'Your dog should make no noise on the peg. He should not jump up at people. He should not steal food. If he does anything good on top of this, it's a bonus!'

Greedy picking up

Just as nobody likes their birds to be 'poached' by their neighbours in the air, they hate it just as much, if not more, if they are poached on the ground by a next-door Gun's greedy dog. Picking up over-zealously on 'their' territory if they have a dog of their own which they are hoping to work, can really cause tempers to fray.

So you have been warned – if you are in any doubt as to whether to take your dog or not, especially if you are hoping to be invited back, then it is best to leave him at home. Though as Janet Menzies observes:

'People love seeing other people's dogs behave badly, it gives them something to talk about and adds a lot of fun and enjoyment to the day! As long as the dog which is bad is also charming, charismatic and attractive, often you will get away with it. If not, you can always cry into its shoulder on the way home.'

In the box opposite there are some useful pointers from the experts to help you avoid those moments of potential disaster.

A gundog mugging

Gundog Dos and Don'ts

Let your dog have a run before the shoot

On arrival, leave your dog in the vehicle

Put your dog on a slip lead when he's not working

At your peg, tie him to a peg or stick

Whining and barking on the peg is not acceptable

Never take a bitch in season out shooting

Apologise if your dog poaches

Do not allow your dog to 'mug' other dogs for their birds

Keep an eye on your dog at all times

Don't let your dog pick up too near the pegs

Keep your dog in the vehicle during elevenses or at lunch

Pickers-up

A real bone of contention is when pickers-up allow their dogs to stray too close to the line before the Guns have had a chance to work their own dogs. The very experienced John Holloway says:

'Any picker-up should leave a decent percentage of easier birds so the Gun can use his dog. But the difficult birds should be picked up straight away. It's a delicate balance. He has got a job to do, but he should also have the good grace to leave a few. As a Gun, if you get the opportunity, then try and find the picker-up before the drive and explain that you want to work your own dog.'

Max Hastings wrote in a recent column for *The Field* that when he admonished a picker-up for straying too close to his peg after a drive, he was told in no uncertain terms: 'I come here to work my dogs, not watch you shoot, you know!' So not all pickers-up see things from the point of view of the Guns.

Apparently the most deadly combination, according to John Holloway, is when a Gun brings his wife to pick up with the dog.

'The best thing she could do, if she wants to pick some birds, is to go with the pickers-up, but she tends to stay with her husband. In most places you don't start picking up until the drive is over, but sometimes, if a runner is going like billy-oh, you do send your dog for it. Well, she sees you do that, and she thinks it's okay to start doing it too and so sends out her dog, and it picks up a bird, then drops it, then picks up another! Oh, it's organised chaos! It is a real source of amusement for us pickers-up, but to be honest, Guns with out of control dogs are a nuisance!'

Any wounded birds falling a long way away must be carefully remembered and their whereabouts explained to a picker-up. With any luck, they will have been marked during the drive, but this can't always be taken for granted. If you have dropped a bird a long way off, it is better to leave it to the professionals rather than attempt to find it yourself. Not only will you delay the next drive if you march off into the distance but you will also be tramping across the scent, making it more difficult for a picker-up to find it later.

Keep count, but never reveal your personal tally

If you truly cannot master the art of marking your birds, at least keep count of the number of birds down. This is not so you can brag about it later. It is considered very bad form to tell your neighbours your personal bag. I was once really surprised, on enquiring how a day's grouse shooting went, to be told 'I got twenty brace'. No mention of the total bag at all, which is what I'd meant! The only person whom you can tell how many you got down is the picker-up. But if you have lost count and say breezily: 'I got loads, no idea how many, not sure where they fell', your words will be met by a steely glare. Having no clue where your birds have landed is seriously irresponsible behaviour – and what separates the true sportsman from an ill-educated slayer. The true sportsman is above all humane, and leaving wounded birds to die a slow death or be devoured by a fox because they cannot fly away, is not something anybody would want.

If the excitement of the drive and the sheer numbers of birds mean that you do completely lose count, whatever you do, always memorise the location of any wounded birds.

If you have a lot of birds lying close to your peg

At the end of the drive, go and pick up those birds lying close to your peg by hand, even if you have a dog, as it will only confuse him and he may pick one, drop it, and go to pick another. Only once you have picked the easier ones must you send him out for the trickier retrieves. Place the birds on your peg or put them in the game cart.

Honour the dead

As I have said, never throw dead game or pile it up. Handle the birds with care. On the continent the dead birds are treated with the utmost respect: they are all lined up at the end of the day and different horns are played to honour them. Everyone removes their hats and takes part in this solemn ritual.

Don't disappear for too long

If you do go off on a solo mission to find a lost bird, remember to alert your host or a neighbouring Gun so that they don't all disappear without you.

One host, a Lincolnshire landowner, is renowned for doing just that. Before he got a gundog of his own, he had no patience with guests disappearing off into the undergrowth to pick up. Sometimes he would just leave behind an errant Gun whose love of working his dog made him lose track of time. The only guide to the where-abouts of the next drive would be a trail of dust as the vehicles drove out of sight. So always keep your eye on your watch and don't expect your host to wait too long.

If you think your host wants to get on, call your dog in and explain to the pickers-up where you think the bird is. Then prepare to leave with the other Guns. Later in the day, it is always polite to enquire whether they found the bird or not, because that shows your interest and appreciation. It also means that the pickers-up will keep an eye out for you and help you during the rest of the day.

Always pick your birds

Helping your neighbours

Shooting is often described as a team sport, and nowhere does this manifest itself quite so much as when you are picking up. While your neighbour might resent any attempt to 'help' him during the drive – by you shooting his birds or finishing them off for him when he has clearly been missing them – after the drive is over, it is another matter. So when you have picked your birds, do offer to help a neighbour with a friendly: 'Are you all picked? Do you need any help?'

Don't claim his birds

To trespass into your neighbour's picking up territory (the area around his peg where most of his birds will have fallen), blatantly helping yourself to his birds and walking

'Has anything been moved?'

off, causes hackles to rise. If one of your birds has fallen into that 'no-man's land' between the two of you, always ask first as to whether he is picked. If he isn't, ask him if he's picked a bird from where you are looking, indicating that you are still missing one. Then just hope that he suggests one of his is in fact yours. Guns get very possessive about their birds, both flying and lying dead, so this is an area fraught with potential danger.

The best advice from one of Britain's most-invited Guns, Jonathan Kennedy, is 'Tread carefully and always let your neighbour claim any bird about which there is any doubt'.

If your neighbour has a dog, and you do too, it is especially crucial that you do not let your dog retrieve anything too close to your neighbour. Everyone wants a few birds for their own dog to retrieve.

Keen shot Nick Fane has some wise words if you are pegged next to someone who insists on claiming all your birds:

> 'If you find yourself drawn next to what I call a "hooverer", a person who comes out of their post like a champagne cork and picks up as many dead birds as he can, as quickly as he can, to adorn his butt, just smile and let him get on with it. At the end of the day, you know exactly what you shot…and so does he. On these big days take a clicker. You can have it quietly in your pocket, no one even has to see it, and it just means that you have a good idea what you have to pick up. Also, if you have shot at a bird at the same time as your neighbour, assume that he has counted it as his and do not add it to your number.'

Wounded birds

On a grouse moor, if it is completely safe to do so, shooting a wounded grouse on the ground is considered just about acceptable, especially if there is a chance the bird will run. Grouse drives are very long and often it is far more humane to shoot a wounded bird on the ground than to let it suffer for the whole length of the drive. However, this would NOT be acceptable on a pheasant or partridge shoot.

If your dog has retrieved a wounded bird, or you have picked one yourself (standing on the tail feathers is quite a good trick if you think it will bolt as you try to pick it up), you need to deal with it immediately. If you always carry with you a 'priest', like those used to kill fish (a small weighted metal truncheon), then you will never be at a loss. A swift blow to the head is the most humane method. Swinging a bird round and round by the neck will often cause the head to fall off and is not to be recommended. If you really cannot despatch a wounded bird efficiently, then hand it over to a picker-up or keeper nearby to do the job for you. In my opinion, it is far better for the bird to be despatched humanely by an expert, than for it to suffer by suffocating slowly at the hands of someone less experienced.

Picking Up Dos and Don'ts

Always pick your birds – not having a dog is no excuse for not doing so

Only pick up your cartridges when you have picked the birds around your peg

If a wounded bird lands very near you during the drive, despatch it immediately

Try to remember how many birds you have shot and mark where they fall

Always be honest about what you have shot

Communicate with the pickers-up

Don't go off on a long picking-up mission without telling your host

Always be generous and let your neighbour claim a disputed bird

Help your neighbour pick up once yours are picked

Always thank the pickers-up at the end of the day

7
The Keeper and the Quarry

'Respect for the quarry is everything. Knowing something of their ways and wiles is fundamental.'
Mike Barnes, editor, *Fieldsports* magazine

It is all too often the case that Guns don't really understand what the keeper's job entails. The sheer grind, day by day, month by month, which goes into making a shoot day possible is frequently underestimated. Many people think that the shooting season is the keeper's 'busy' time, when in fact by far the most gruelling is the rearing season. Some of those who shoot would have a lot more respect for the keeper if they knew a little more about what the job involves.

Similarly keepers always appreciate a Gun who shows a basic understanding and knowledge of what their work really entails. John Pyle, head keeper for eighteen years at a pheasant and partridge shoot in the north of England, confirms this:

'People often say to me on shoot days, "Oh, this must be your busiest time of year", but actually it's out of the shooting season that we are busiest. What a lot of people don't realise is that the rearing season is by far the hardest time of year. I probably do fifteen hours a day, seven days a week from April until September. My day starts at 4.30am in April/May time, as I go to the rearing sheds and let the birds out into their runs. You have to check them constantly all day and I check them last thing at night too.'

A low ground keeper's year:

January: Shoot days continue throughout January, although by now birds may be getting a little scarcer. The traditional Keepers' Day held at the end of January usually heralds the end of the season, which is 1 February. On this day, the entire regular shoot staff get a chance to shoot, by way of thanks for all their help during the season. Often they take turns beating and shooting, and sometimes the beating line will be armed to stop the cannier birds flying back. Shoots which rear their own birds won't shoot any hens because they are needed for catching up later for laying.

February/March: Keepers will be mainly employed catching up hens for laying, clearing the rides and repairing release pens. Vermin control, particularly fox lamping, is a key part of the job at this time of year. As this is the quietest time for a keeper, he will often take his annual holiday now.

April/May: The pressure is on! The hatching and rearing season begins. Many estates no longer hatch their own birds because it is incredibly time-consuming and expensive. Those that do will have caught up as many hens as possible and the eggs are collected several times a day and placed in incubators. They need to be checked continually which is very time consuming. Incubators now are state-of-the-art and very expensive to run, and also need to be replaced every few years. It is often less costly for estates to buy in birds as day-olds, and then nurture them in heated rearing sheds, shutting them up at night, and letting them into their 'day-run' in the early morning. This is when a keeper is working the hardest, he is up at 4.30 or 5.00am most days, and there is no such thing as a day off or the birds will simply die. He needs to check the rearing sheds several times a day, constantly topping up feed and water.

June/July: The birds are now six-week-old poults and are put into the release pens in the woods, having first had their flight feathers trimmed to avoid them simply flying away. These feathers will re-grow in a few weeks, but by this time the poults will have acclimatised to life in the release pens and will come to regard them as 'home'. They need to be fed first thing in the morning and last thing at night, and have a plentiful supply of water. The keeper will have to keep a close eye out for any foxes which may attempt to get into the release pens and many a night will be spent lamping. They will also have to be very wary of poachers who may steal young poults and sell them off to other shoots. Vermin control is on-going and on wild shoots, where no rearing is done, constant vigilance is needed as the hens are so vulnerable nesting on the ground.

July/August: The poults are released into the wild completely, with the lower part of their release pen being raised so the birds can familiarise themselves with the local territory. Technically they are free to roam wherever they want but by now the pens are considered as 'home'. Throughout the shooting season they will always return to roost there.

If the shoot also rears partridge, they arrive as ten-week-old poults at around this time; they are put in sheds with sectional runs to start with and released in August.

September/October: Partridge shooting starts on 1 September, and the whole cycle begins again. Prior to the first shoot day, about a month before, the keeper will have to organise all the beaters, flankers and pickers-up he will need that season. He will have a huge list of people to telephone and will give them all the shoot dates. The sheer organisational skills of a keeper in the run up to a shoot day must not be underestimated: someone will always drop out at the last minute, and, if it's a big double-gun day, he will often have to book the loaders as well. Some of the best pickers-up will obviously be in demand from several shoots and again, finding them all is down to the keeper.

October/November/December: The shooting season is in full swing. Some estates have one or two shoots each week, whilst some of the larger ones will shoot six days out of seven.

Not all keepers enjoy the actual running of a shoot day and the interaction with the Guns, but head keeper John Pyle who runs forty shooting days a season, is very relaxed.

'I never worry about a shoot day, as a general rule I don't get stressed, but just running a team of thirty or more people is quite a thing! The hardest thing is when a team of Guns who've been coming for a long time start to specify exactly which drives they want. They may say: "We want the same drives as we had last time" but the weather conditions may be completely different.'

Grouse moor keepers

'Why are grouse so much more expensive to shoot than pheasants, when you don't even have to rear them?' This was a question overheard from a foreign Gun before a day's grouse shooting. Anyone who thinks a grouse keeper has a cushy job compared to a pheasant or partridge keeper is hugely mistaken. He may not have to tend to the needs of penned birds at all hours of the day, but he must be constantly vigilant for vermin, especially foxes. After talking to several grouse keepers I have concluded that sleeping is not something they do very much. Their day starts very early and often they work right through the night. Checking trap lines on their 'beat', anything up to 3,000 acres or more, can take a keeper all day, and no sooner has he finished, than he has to start again. Heather burning, a vital part of successful moor management, also takes a lot of time – ten per cent of the moor needs to be burned in small patches each year, to ensure regular heather regeneration. Young grouse feed mainly on new heather shoots. Regular repairs to roads and butts must also be fitted in, as well as the construction of new butts.

Jonathan Kennedy knows about both grouse moors and grouse keepers. His firm has acted for the buyer or seller of more than fifteen grouse moors in the past twenty years, including Gunnerside, East Allenheads, Stanhope and Wemmergill. He says:

'Grouse keepers are exceptional people – they make or break a moor. The best hill keepers are worth their weight in gold and the best owners appreciate that. To do the job really well requires energy and passion. But the rewards of top quality hill keepering are invariably demonstrated clearly by the sheer quantity of grouse. No excuses are required when the keepering is right.'

Hatching time

If the weather is cold and wet at hatching time, a keeper's year-long work can be destroyed by the wrong weather at the wrong time. Desmond Coates, head keeper at Grinton, North Yorkshire, for Willie Peel, says:

'My favourite time of year is hatching time, which is about 21 May onwards. I love seeing everything come to fruition; it's the accumulation of all the hours of work I've put in. I can't lie in bed, I get up at 4am and just go and watch them.'

Each brood is marked on a map and the keepers work round the clock to protect them against predators. If a keeper sees that suddenly a brood of eleven has shrunk to five, he will do everything he can to find out what has happened, and defend his grouse. Against the weather, though, he can do nothing. Broods can usually cope with wet weather, or cold, but both together are a fatal combination.

Every day is different

Paul Simpson, a head keeper in North Yorkshire says:

> 'There's no such thing as a "normal" day, that's the great thing about being a grouse keeper, every day is different. There is no set time to get up, and sometimes I'll have been out lamping or dosing all night… But on a normal bog standard day, I would get up at 6am. It's constant vigilance, for rooks, stoats, rats, and hooded crows. If there's a fox, and it is the height of summer, I will get up before daylight, 3am, and go and sit somewhere and just wait.'

Paul has been head keeper for thirteen years now, and his moor broke its best ever record in 2008. The qualities he believes all keepers need, but in particular grouse keepers, are lots of energy, enthusiasm and self-motivation. He continues:

> 'You can't get away with anything. It's easier to get away with things than if you are rearing birds, but at the end of the day, you just can't, because it will show in the bags. It's a seven-day-a-week job. It's unpredictable, but not as tying as rearing birds when you cannot miss a single day or you will start to lose birds… When I first started as head keeper I was mad keen, I would be out lamping foxes all night, five nights a week. Now it's more like two nights a week, but my under-keeper will be out four or five nights a week.'

Fox damage

What all grouse keepers have in common is an absolute intolerance of foxes on their moors. When you think how vulnerable the hen grouse is you realise why. If a fox takes a hen off the nest, then the whole clutch of eggs is lost. In the July counts, if you see just cock grouse getting up and no hens, then you know that there has been fox damage.

Every ten to twelve days in the spring and early summer, grouse keepers will walk the entire moor, four to eight keepers in a line depending on the size of the moor, to search for signs of fox cubs. Paul says: 'We check every rabbit hole which they could have dug out, every bit of woodland, literally anywhere a fox could be. We don't sleep; we are out *all* the time.'

Keepers are key conservationists

The important conservation work which grouse keepers do is often totally unappreciated by locals and misunderstood by the wider public. Desmond says:

'I get sick of keepers being viewed as the scourge of the community – the public think we are murderers! But if it wasn't for our work, you wouldn't get the huge numbers of ground nesting birds, such as curlews, lapwings and golden plovers which all come up here to breed. Even merlin (small falcons) nest in long heather and are just as vulnerable to fox predation. As a result of our work, the moor is alive with wildlife, especially in the early summer.'

A grouse keeper's year:

January/February: The start of the year sees grouse keepers focusing, as normal, on vermin control. Snares and traps will be checked regularly. At night they will be busy lamping for foxes. Gritting stations need to be continually monitored and kept well supplied. Grit is vital for the grouse to digest the heather, and medicated grit helps guard against worms. Some moors now 'direct dose', which is a way of catching a grouse and administering a worming medicine orally. It can only be done at night and is incredibly time-consuming. It is most effective on moors where certain patches are suffering from high worm densities.

March: Heather burning takes place this month. You need a quick, cool fire, with a bit of a wind, so it goes over the ground faster. Often Argocats with sprayers (kind of power-washes which come out of the sides) are used to control the fire, which is far better than the old-fashioned method of beating it with 'floggers' or 'besoms' as they are more correctly known. There is a huge amount of new legislation governing the amount and location of each burning strip which causes great resentment amongst keepers who are more often than not experts on the subject but now have to abide by a myriad of rules.

April: The grouse are beginning to nest by mid-April. Keepers will redouble their vermin-control efforts, laying trap lines, and checking these as well as keeping a lookout for foxes. This is the important time to keep a relentless vigilance for vermin.

May/June: Checking trap lines and vermin control, fox lamping around the clock. The chicks are starting to hatch by the end of May and are at their most vulnerable to predators and bad weather. Keepers are starting to get ready for the new season and will be busy repairing roads and butts. It can take two men three or four days to build a stone butt from scratch. They are works of art! A friend who worked as a grouse keeper for a year said that when he was learning the art of butt-building, the head keeper would take a run at a new one to see if he could knock it down or whether it stood the test.

July: The July counts take place now. The keepers will count the number of hens and broods, plus how many are in each brood, per square mile of the estate. The counting is crucial for establishing how many days shooting should be planned in order to be left with a good sustainable stock of birds.

August: Start of the season – 12 August. The traditional school of thought is that half the bag should be shot in August. (Later in the season, weather conditions may deteriorate, and also it can be impossible to drive the birds over the butts as they become 'butt-shy'.) As with all shooting, arranging shoot days is very time-consuming, as the keeper has to ensure he has the correct number of beaters, flankers, pickers-up and loaders. There is always stiff competition from other moors to find enough staff.

September/October: More shoot days will be planned. Continuing vermin control. Some keepers may be asked to go and load elsewhere for their boss or on neighbouring estates, as everyone helps each other out on shoot days.

November/December: By now the grouse will have 'packed up' (i.e. be flying together in huge coveys or packs) and be extremely difficult to drive over the Guns. In most years, all shooting will have finished by now, but if there are large stocks left, then more shoot days will be arranged. Often at this time of year any keepers in the beating line will carry guns to try and cull the birds going back. Leaving too great a stock of birds is a serious problem and can lead to disease.

The end of the season is 10 December. Around this time a Keepers' Day is often laid on to thank all the shoot staff for their help. As Paul Simpson says:

> 'A lot of estates these days recognise that not all those who come out to help, shoot! There are a lot of women involved now, and they don't tend to shoot. So at the end of the season we always put on an evening for everyone in the local pub, put £500 behind the bar and give everyone drinks and sausage and chips. It's a great way to end the season.'

Knowing your birds

As well as some knowledge of the keeper's role, the ideal shooting guest will have an understanding of and appreciation for the species he is shooting. Unlike our European contemporaries, in Britain we do not have to pass any written test in order to obtain the right to shoot driven birds. Once you have been granted a shotgun certificate and the firearms officer has checked your gun is stored safely, you can set forth to shoot with no further ado. Even the old-fashioned game licence which you used to have to purchase from the post office has been abolished, except in Scotland.

In Europe, 'hunters', as they are called, are incredibly well-informed about all aspects of wildlife. They can identify a bird of prey from miles away, recognise the

Knowing your birds

different mating sounds of roe deer, and are fully conversant with the breeding cycles and habitat of their quarry. In the UK though it is entirely possible that a new Gun could arrive on the shooting field having not the slightest clue as to how to tell the difference between a thrush, a blackbird and a partridge. He may well believe that partridges nest in trees. As Mike Barnes, editor of *Fieldsports* magazine says:

> 'Respect for the quarry is everything. We are not simply shooting targets – pheasants and partridges are for real. Knowing something of their ways and wiles is fundamental. As is knowing fully how a shooting day works. It also adds so much to the enjoyment of time spent in the field.'

Having a good working knowledge of both habitat and species, as well as the work that has gone into making the day possible, makes a lot of sense if you are going to take up shooting. Like anything, the more you know about a subject, the more you get out of it and it will add a whole new dimension to your shooting day if you are aware of at least the basics.

I strongly recommend every aspiring game shot to get hold of a copy of the BASC Quarry Identification Guide, which contains a brief description of all the main game bird species as well as many wildfowl, with a photograph of each in flight. (Download it from the internet at www.basc.org.uk/content/quarry_identification_guide). There is also a section on pest species which a responsible Gun should be able to recognise.

What follows here is not an in-depth guide to game bird species, but an outline of the basic facts which is intended to enrich your whole experience of shooting. Though some may find it heavy going, others will find it interesting.

The pheasant

Pheasants are thought to have been brought over to Italy from Asia by the Romans and then to the UK. There is evidence of them being around in 350 AD. They were shot and highly prized as game birds from as early as the eighteenth century and some of the big estates in the Edwardian age were rearing 12,000 birds a year. However, pheasant rearing really got into its stride across Britain by the 1960s when wild partridges declined in great numbers due to intensive farming and pesticides. The pheasant now accounts for eighty per cent of all game birds shot in the UK.

Pheasants roost up in trees at night but nest on the ground. They eat seeds, fruits, green shoots, leaves, insects, earthworms, slugs etc. Reared birds are mostly fed on grain (wheat) or specially milled pellets. The hen, which is the plainer looking of the two, is heavily camouflaged because it is she who does most of the rearing of the young. The cock bird, whose plumage is so bright and exuberant, has barely any paternal instincts and enjoys a harem of different hens, scaring off any unwanted male rivals. Cock pheasants are very territorial and won't allow any other male to enter their territory in the mating season, and even before.

A hen in the wild usually lays about twelve to fifteen eggs. She will barely leave the nest at all, often losing a lot of condition at this time. She may only leave for a few minutes in the evening to feed and drink, and if her nest is disturbed she won't return. It takes twenty-four days for the eggs to hatch and when they do, it is vital that the chicks have a plentiful supply of insects to eat and that they do not get too wet or cold. The combination of wet and cold is fatal to any young chick and a whole brood can die if these conditions persist for longer than a day or two. A fox in the neighbourhood can lay waste to huge numbers of nesting hens and their eggs in a single night, so these and other vermin, such as rats, stoats, weasels and magpies must always be kept in check on any shooting estate.

Few shoots now rely solely on wild pheasants. Many believe that wild pheasant shooting is unsurpassable but there are only a handful of days available per season.

On the whole, in the UK the pheasant is a reared game bird. The majority of them are bred in France and then imported. The chicks start 'colouring up' at around five weeks of age, which means you can already tell which is a cock and which is a

'After you. No please, after YOU.'

hen. As we have seen, they are kept in rearing sheds until the age of about six weeks, being carefully monitored several times a day, and then released in pens in woods, where they are well looked after and protected from any predators.

Shooting pheasant

Season: 1 October – 1 February

Not much shooting takes place until the end of October and in most places the beginning of November heralds the start of the pheasant season proper. Around 25 million birds are reared annually in the UK and will be about six or seven months old when they are first put over the Guns. A pheasant, although far larger and heavier than a partridge, does actually fly much faster: it can accelerate very quickly from take-off but cannot sustain this effort for very long. The wing beats last for only about ten seconds followed by gliding which sustains the bird's speed. If a shoot is well-run, and planted out in such a way that the pheasant is flying 'home', a pheasant can fly very high and keep climbing on a direct path. It is vital that the birds don't expend too much energy when being driven by the beaters, from an area where they will have been feeding, to return to the home wood or covert. A well-run team of beaters won't whoop and shout which would frighten the birds unnecessarily into flying too early. The experts tell me that just a gentle tapping will encourage the bird to run, until such a point that it will take off in exactly the right place – known as the flushing point. With the Guns placed correctly, the bird will be climbing very steeply and thus provide a very sporting shot. It is easy to see why it is such a popular game bird.

The partridge

Grey (English) partridge

The grey partridge is indigenous to the UK. A ground nesting bird, the wild grey is smaller than its red-legged counterpart; it has declined in huge numbers since the 1960s with the advent of modern farming techniques. The grey favours the sandy soil of East Anglia. Some of the largest wild grey partridge shoots are based in Norfolk, and an invitation to shoot wild greys at Holkham is bound to cause great excitement for any shooting person. Also known as an English partridge, the grey used to form the main species of game bird shot in the UK. Prior to the 1960s, around two million of them were shot each year without any reduction of the future stock, which gives some idea of how plentiful they once were across the whole of Britain.

In order to thrive the wild grey needs good cover and vermin control, and a plentiful supply of food. They like grasslands, set-aside and hedges, and feed on seeds, particularly seeds of plants which modern farming terms as weeds. Such plants in fact carry the insects which are the primary diet of partridge chicks. Shoots hoping to increase their stocks of wild greys have to be very intensively keepered as the partridge is very vulnerable to predators, especially foxes.

English partridge normally start to pair up in February (though it can be as early as December) and they usually stay together unless one of them dies. They make very good parents and as many as ninety per cent of their eggs will hatch. They can lay more than twenty. Mid-June is when the chicks first appear and for the first ten days of their lives they eat mostly insects.

French or red-legged partridge

As a rule, shoots which rear partridges tend to rear red-legs, or French partridge rather than greys. This is because the 'Frenchies', as they are also referred to, are hardier birds and are better equipped to survive the hard winters in the UK and most importantly, are less likely to stray.

A red-legged partridge chick is for some reason not quite so dependent on insects in their first few days so they do survive better as a rearing bird because they eat corn from a young age. Red-legs in the wild will lay clutches of ten to fifteen eggs from late April to May. Usually the eggs will be laid in two nests, with the father raising one brood.

Shoots rearing large numbers of red-leg partridges won't see much improvement in the stock of wild greys, despite best efforts at habitat improvement and vermin control. This is because the wild grey is very territorial and won't stick around in areas where there are too many other partridges. You will sometimes see them, but they are an increasingly rare sight.

Shooting partridge

Season: 1 September – 1 February

Wild greys will almost literally 'explode' over a hedge in a covey and can take you completely by surprise, whereas red-leg partridges tend to come over in ones and twos. If you are shooting traditional partridges, at hedge height, it can be rather a shock if you are used to shooting pheasants, and can feel very unsafe. Many Guns prefer to shoot them much higher. However, it is perfectly safe if you know what you are doing: never shoot *through* a hedge and always know exactly where the beaters, pickers-up and flankers are.

French partridges provide a wonderful variety of sport and are extremely popular throughout the country – the season is long and enables shoots to extend their season by almost two months, which spreads overheads substantially. Partridges can be presented over a multitude of different types of terrain; you can see them star-bursting over the hedges of a traditional East Anglian partridge shoot, gliding over high hedges and the deep chalk valleys of the south of England or rocketing off the best topography that the north of England or the West Country has to offer.

One thing to bear in mind is that partridges have very good hearing. Guns should be aware that loud chatting or door slamming could spoil a drive. This is especially the case if shooting wild partridge.

The grouse

The grouse is indigenous to Britain and unique to the British Isles. It is larger than a partridge, dark reddish brown in colour, measuring about sixteen inches in length and has white feather-clad feet. Grouse habitat is the rugged heather moorland of the north of England and Scotland, situated at altitudes between 500 and 3,000 feet. Grouse used to be plentiful in Wales but they have nearly all gone now and predators such as buzzards and red kites abound. Grouse were once to be found in good numbers on Exmoor but to find one anywhere else other than the north is now extremely unusual.

A friend of mine's mother, Barbara Hawkins, a fabulous shot, decided to play a trick on a friend out shooting about thirty years ago. She placed a pre-warmed grouse behind a very famous shot in Staffordshire who picked it, was astounded, and went on to tell everyone about his feat! He wrote to *The Times* and *Country Life* and was even, reputedly, interviewed by the press. Having dined out on the story for a long time it was rather embarrassing for him twenty years later when he discovered the truth. Barbara was never asked again!

A grouse's diet consists mainly of young heather shoots but it will also eat alternative food such as bilberries and crowberries. A plentiful supply of grit is needed to aid their digestion and on well-keepered moors you will find gritting stations criss-crossing the whole moor.

The grouse is widely regarded as the one truly wild game bird left in any large numbers, since the demise of the partridge in the 1960s. Numerous attempts have been made to rear grouse but none have been terribly successful. The only way to produce good stocks of grouse is sheer hard grind, good heather management, lots of highly motivated and energetic young keepers, and, most important of all, non-stop vermin control. It also helps to have well-tended, small numbers of sheep. All this takes a lot of money, time and devotion. Grouse nest on the ground so are in constant danger from all manner of vermin, especially foxes, stoats and wild cats which can decimate several young broods in a day. Crows, rooks and magpies are also on the keeper's hit list as they eat eggs and fledglings.

It takes twenty-two days for the hen to hatch a clutch of eggs. She starts sitting either at the beginning or middle of April, and she won't lay an egg a day, she may lay one egg, then miss a day, then lay two more. It can take her fifteen or sixteen days to lay a clutch of ten eggs, but they will all hatch together. As soon as they hatch the chicks are off, and they are already pecking at heather buds in the first few days. Hen grouse are unbelievably good mothers, and the cock grouse helps rear the young too. If a hen gets killed, the cock will try to rear the young himself. I am told no other game bird will do this.

People talk about 'a good year for the grouse' and get very excited about it if it is a good year. This is because so much can go wrong with them – they are the most unpredictable type of game bird and no one ever takes a good grouse season for granted. Their elusiveness adds to the sense of excitement when an invitation to shoot them comes through your letterbox. Right from the start, if the weather is cold and wet at hatching time, broods will suffer huge mortality rates.

Some moors are plagued with louping ill, a tick-borne disease carried by sheep and deer (and in Scotland, mountain hares). Bracken harbours the ticks, which brush off on to the animal as it passes and the virus can then be passed on to the grouse. Having a lot of bracken on a grouse moor is a very bad sign and most owners spend fortunes spraying it off, if they can afford to do so.

Grouse are also prone to a parasitic worm (strongylosis), which colonises the birds' gut, depleting them of vital nutrients. When these worms are present in large numbers, birds are literally starved to death. Thus infected many birds don't survive the winter and the hens which do can die on the nest so that whole broods just never hatch. It is important for moor owners to leave a stock of good healthy birds but not too many, as this will lead to disease and a poor following season.

If you are, or hope to become, a keen grouse shot, then a basic knowledge of these illnesses is an important part of understanding grouse moor management. This will enable you to appreciate properly the sheer grind that goes into making a day's grouse shooting possible.

Shooting grouse

Season: 12 August – 10 December

Although the season continues from the 'Glorious Twelfth' (of August) right through to 10 December, other than in a very good year little shooting takes place after the end of October. August grouse are probably the easiest to shoot as they fly low, straight at the butts, hugging the contours of the ground. Nearer the end of the season the birds become butt-shy and jink away.

The woodcock

Part of the wader family, the woodcock is much prized as a game bird. It is quite small, in fact quite a bit smaller than a partridge. It is well camouflaged in dark browns with light shades underneath. Largely nocturnal, its eyes sit so far back on its head that the woodcock can see all around, including behind itself.

Some 740,000 woodcock migrate to the UK in small flocks landing mainly on the eastern coastline from Aberdeen to Folkestone. They are rarely seen in the south west. They tend to arrive in October or November from their breeding grounds in Russia, Finland and Scandinavia. But there is a small resident breeding population, of just under 80,000 pairs. Woodcock thrive in damp woodland and heath land. They spend most of the day in dense cover in woodland, hidden on the wood floor perfectly blended with dead leaves by their camouflage pattern of broken black and brown feathers. At dusk they come out into the fields to feed. A woodcock can open its beak just at the tip as it probes deep into soft soil, and it is specially shaped to enable the bird to grasp earthworms, its favourite food, and pull them from the soil. Woodcock also eat beetles, spiders, caterpillars, fly larvae and small snails.

The distinctive courtship flight of the male woodcock is called 'roding' and is usually performed in the twilight just before dawn and at dusk. The bird flies in circles with a flickering flight high above the canopy with its bill held point downwards and makes a series of croaking sounds ending with a sharp squeak. The sounds can be heard from a long way away.

The hen woodcock lays four eggs in a shallow dip on the ground, often under bushes, amongst dead leaves and twigs. The eggs are a beautifully camouflaged brown-spotted colour. The hen incubates the eggs for about twenty-one days. Birds may re-nest if the nest is destroyed or if the young are lost early during brood rearing. The male woodcock gives no parental care, but continues to display long after most females have laid their eggs.

Unlike many birds that leave their nests at hatching, newly hatched woodcock cannot feed themselves. They are dependent on the mother for food for the first week although the chicks start to probe in the soil three or four days after hatching. The young will huddle under the hen for warmth during the first ten days.

Before they are truly independent, the young are vulnerable to death from cold, wet weather. The hen's mothering tapers off after three weeks, and the young are on their own after about thirty-five days, when they will leave the brooding area but remain nearby until migration time in the spring.

Shooting woodcock

Season: 1 October – 31 January

Most people who shoot in the UK will have seen the odd woodcock fly over the line in their characteristic 'zigzag' way during a pheasant drive, but few will have been on a driven woodcock day. Such days are extremely rare and you are honoured indeed to be invited to one. The Western Isles of Scotland, such as Lewis, and the west of Northern Ireland are right on the migratory flight path so numbers are more plentiful here.

Barons Court in County Tyrone offers some amazing driven woodcock days. Resident agent Robert Scott says:

> 'We manage the largest forestry estate in Northern Ireland, 4,000 acres, of which half is in hand and half leased to the Forest Service. We manage the forest with woodcock in mind and create wide "rides" which increase the "edge effect" making the habitat more hospitable to woodcock as it allows more shelter and light into the wood, which benefits many other species as well.'

Woodcock are tremendously difficult birds to shoot, as they jink and swoop just as you pull the trigger, and can tempt excitable Guns to take unsafe shots. Driven days are very unusual and very exciting. The birds come out of the wood at different heights, speeds and angles and this is definitely not a day for beginners. You have to have sharp reflexes and a sharp eye as woodcock are well camouflaged against the woodland and fly noiselessly.

The size of each bag depends on external and climatic factors that vary from year to year. Incidentally, if you ever get the chance to shoot a right and left at woodcock and succeed, you can join the Woodcock Club. The criteria are strict and you need to have had the deed witnessed by two people. In days gone by the club was sponsored by the Dutch Bols liqueur company, but in 1983 *Shooting Times* took over the organisation of the club, with sponsorship from J&B Whiskey. There is an annual black tie dinner and the chairman is Sir Nicholas Soames. When asked if he'd ever had the opportunity to shoot a right and left of woodcock he replied, 'I always hope to have the chance to do so, although I think it is likely that the woodcock would come off better.' Because of the whole prestige of belonging to the Woodcock Club, it is naturally considered the worst possible sin to shoot the left of someone's potential right and left.

Incidentally, if you are a guest on a mixed day and you shoot a woodcock, don't take it for granted that your host will let you take the bird home with you. He may be partial to woodcock himself. Wait to be offered the bird before helping yourself.

The snipe

The Latin name is *Gallinago gallinago* and the snipe, or common snipe, as it is also known, is part of the wader family. Its closest relative is the woodcock, but it looks a bit like a scaled down version of a woodcock, with slightly paler brown feathers. Another way to distinguish the two if you are not sure (but obviously you can't see this when about to shoot one!) is that snipe have head stripes going across the top of the crown rather than along it, unlike the woodcock. Both sexes are mottled brown, with paler buff stripes on the back and dark streaks on the chest and pale under parts. Snipe are declining in many areas, because wet meadows have been drained and converted to arable land or to improved grassland. The largest concentration of breeding snipe is to be found on the Ouse Washes. The population varies, but has been as high as 370 pairs during recent summers. Conservation bodies have increased their holdings of wet meadowland but reserves can only hope to save a small amount of what existed formerly. Snipe face serious problems when their habitat deteriorates because these birds feed by feeling for their prey deep in the soil with their long beaks. If the marshes and meadows are well drained – or were not waterlogged at the end of the winter – then the ground may become dry and hard and breeding will cease. The birds search for invertebrates in the mud with a 'sewing machine' action of their long bills.

In spring, snipe perform spectacular displays high in the sky. Each male, following a circular route, makes a series of power dives during which the outermost tail-feathers are held out almost at right-angles to the bird's body. Feather vibration in the slipstream produces the remarkable throbbing known as 'drumming', which takes place throughout the breeding season. Once a female snipe is attracted the male pursues her and dives with wings held above the body in a v-shape, often rolling and turning upside-down.

The male takes no part in incubation, continuing drumming displays over the nesting territory. He feeds mostly at night, spending much of the day resting in cover.

Many breeding attempts fail. Crows or stoats may take the eggs, while trampling by livestock and late flooding are also hazards. Fortunately snipe are persistent breeders and females may produce three or four clutches in the season before managing to rear young. In these circumstances the latest nests may be started in July.

Shooting snipe

Season: 12 August – 31 January
Snipe fly very erratically, often quite high, and it takes a lot of skill to bring them down. Indeed the difficulty of shooting them gave rise to the term 'sniper', referring to a skilled military sharpshooter.

That said, they are quite a small bird, so if you do hit one it will take only one or two pellets to bring it down. Good marking is essential because a lot of gundogs refuse to retrieve them. Worryingly for the game shot, the common snipe looks very similar to a Jack Snipe, which is protected in England and Scotland, but not Northern Ireland. To avoid confusion, the Jack Snipe is much smaller, with a shorter beak, and rarely gathers enough height actually to fly over the Guns, although you never know. If in doubt, just don't shoot! Many people prefer not to shoot snipe at all, as they are becoming such a rare sight.

Wildfowl

There are many different kinds of duck which can be legally shot in the UK. Of them all, mallard is by far the most common. But you can also shoot: teal, wigeon (also spelt widgeon), tufted, pochard, shoveller, pintail and gadwall. If you go duck-flighting you really need to mug up on what each looks like, especially when in flight, so that you don't make a mistake and shoot a protected bird such as an avocet which is the RSPB's emblem and now very rare.

Wildfowl inhabit wetland areas, in particular estuaries and marshes, as well as small ponds and rivers. They usually feed by dabbling for plant food or grazing; there are reports of mallard eating frogs. They are all ground-nesting birds, usually on riverbanks or near estuaries, and as such are very vulnerable to fox predation. As well as plants and insects, small fish and shell-fish, they also eat seeds, acorns and berries. All wildfowl are very partial to corn, in particular wheat, so if you want them on your land, you need to feed them. John Plumptre, who owns 2,000 acres of North Kent marshland says:

> 'You've got to try and make your land like a five-star hotel for ducks. They need fresh water, so you need to dig large drainage ditches, of the right depth, with shallower parts at the edges. It also helps if you feed them, on demand, every day. To have a keeper watching out for foxes and other predators is also beneficial.'

All species differ slightly in their breeding habits, so I will outline the usual behaviour of the mallard, which is the most common type of wildfowl which the average Gun will be shooting.

Mallard form pairs only until the female lays eggs, at which time she is left by the male. The clutch is eight to thirteen eggs, which are incubated for twenty-seven to twenty-eight days to hatching with fifty to sixty days to fledging. The best time to see ducklings is at the end of May or early June. The ducklings are 'precocial', which means they can swim and feed themselves on insects as soon as they hatch, although they stay near the female for protection.

When they pair off with mating partners, one or several drakes will end up 'left out'. This group will sometimes target an isolated female duck – chasing, pestering and pecking at her until she weakens, often referred to by researchers as 'rape flight'. Male mallard will also occasionally chase other males in the same way.

Shooting duck

Season: 1 September – 31 January (inland), – 20 February (foreshore)

Mallard are easy to rear and many pheasant shoots start the day off with a duck drive. The worst kind of duck drives are when tame duck endlessly circle their 'home' pond and as they come lower and lower, they make quite easy shooting. This is not very sporting and bears no relation to the truly challenging sport of duck-flighting.

Sitting in a hide in your balaclava on the foreshore at first light, with your weighted decoys bobbing about in the water upwind of you as you wait for the duck to come in, is one of the most exciting experiences a keen shot can have. The UK has huge numbers of duck living on its many estuaries by day, coming inland to rest up at night. If you are lucky, in a day you can shoot around eight or nine different species of duck. As well as decoys, another trick wild-fowlers have for attracting duck are different 'duck-calling' whistles. You can get a teal call, a wigeon whistle or a pintail whistle or mallard bellows. (But don't try and put all these round your neck at once because it makes shooting rather tricky!)

Since 1999 it has been illegal to shoot duck or waders with lead shot. There are various alternatives available: tin, which is considered far too soft, and steel, which is regarded by many as too hard, and ruins the barrels of a good English gun. It also seems to go straight through the duck and out the other side, which results in more wounding than clean kills. Another option is Tungsten Matrix, and also bismuth, which are preferable to tin or steel, but each cartridge will set you back just under £1. A new version, called Hevi-Shot, is even more expensive, at £1.25 per cartridge.

Winged vermin to shoot on a driven day

If you get a chance to shoot any of the following on a driven day, the keeper will be delighted. There is no close season so they can be shot all year round and you will amass instant brownie-points. However you must know how to identify the different species of winged vermin you are likely to see on a shoot day: whatever you do, don't confuse a blackbird with a jay, or a sparrow hawk with a wood pigeon. If you are genuinely unsure which bird it is, don't shoot. (A well-known Gun recently shot a peregrine falcon by mistake, which was retrieved by a labrador belonging to the local chief of police who was out picking up that day…)

Crows
Black all over, with black beaks, they feast on freshly killed corpses and have been known to kill weak lambs. They also eat eggs which is why keepers loathe them. Commonly known as carrion crows, these are part of the corvid family, comprising rooks and jays. They are known to be extremely clever – tests have shown that they top the scale of avian intelligence! They rarely come right over the Guns as they know exactly what's going on. Usually they are seen only as solitary birds or in pairs.

Rooks
Once you know how to distinguish a rook from a crow, you'll never get it wrong: a rook is slightly smaller than a carrion crow, its head is more peaked, and they have paler, thinner beaks. They are also far more sociable and not likely to be seen on their own. They roost in flocks in trees, often with jackdaws. They too eat eggs, so are the scourge of keepers.

Magpies
Most people can identify a magpie! But just in case: their head, breast and back and wings are black, their belly and flanks are white. The tail accounts for over half the total length of the bird and they have an unmistakable 'chacker-chacker' call. They eat insects, rodents, carrion, grains and berries, and eggs and nestlings too. They are incredibly difficult to shoot and are usually far too wily to fly over the line, though sometimes a young one might not be so wary. If one does fly out amongst the pheasants or partridges, it is good form to focus on killing the magpie rather than the game bird.

Jays

The jay is a colourful crow. It is mostly pinkish brown, with paler under parts, with black and white flecked crown and a white throat. Its tail and wings are mostly black with white patches, but they also have striking blue patches. They are very sociable birds and have many different calls; they can even imitate other birds. The male and female mate for life.

They feed on acorns, beech mast, fruits, insects, small rodents, bats, newts, bird eggs and young birds. Some people say they are oak-planters and their benefits as such outweigh the fact that they eat eggs. But most keepers would shoot them on sight and most shoots would want you to do the same if one came over the line.

Wood pigeons

Part of the *Columbidae* family, the wood pigeon is the UK's largest and commonest pigeon. It is largely grey with a pinkish breast, a white neck patch and white wing patches which are clearly visible in flight. Although shy in the countryside it can be tame and approachable in towns and cities. Its cooing call is a familiar sound in woodlands as is the loud clatter of its wings when it flies away. The wood pigeon is gregarious, often forming very large flocks outside the breeding season. A resident UK bird, it is mostly sedentary though in the autumn and winter it flies twice daily between roosts and feeding areas.

As the name suggests, wood pigeons inhabit woodland, but they are also found across the UK in fields as well as in towns and cities where they frequent parks and gardens. They feed on crops like wheat, barley, cabbages and sprouts, and are especially partial to peas. They are a particular pest to peas, because the crop is vulnerable at every stage of its growth. They will also eat buds, shoots, grass seeds, beech mast, nuts and berries. They also drink a lot, mainly because they do not get sufficient moisture from their food, unlike birds that eat earthworms. An interesting feature of the way they drink is that they use their beaks like a straw, whereas other birds scoop the water up and throw their heads back to let it flow down their throats.

At breeding time wood pigeons can be seen 'displaying'. They fly upwards, clap their wings, and then glide downwards with tail spread. Wood pigeons breed in trees in woods, parks and gardens, laying two white eggs in a simple stick nest, which is curiously unsophisticated and the white eggs lie exposed with no attempt to camouflage them at all. The parents will take it in turn to guard the nest and the eggs hatch after seventeen to nineteen days. They seem to have a preference for trees near roadways and rivers. Their nests are vulnerable to attack, particularly by crows; the more so early in the year when the leaf cover is not fully formed and the eggs are very visible in the nest. They do better in areas that are well keepered and numbers of crows and magpies are kept in check. The young usually fly at thirty-three to thirty-four days; however if the nest is disturbed some young may be able to survive having left the nest as early as twenty days after hatching. You will find young pigeons on the wing on every month throughout the year.

Shooting wood pigeons is extremely sporting and some game shots are addicted to the sport. Because they are classed as agricultural pests, in the same way as corvids, shooting them is actually doing the farmer a favour so it can be a very inexpensive form of extremely exciting shooting. Wood pigeons can be shot under an EU general licence, which means that numbers can be controlled in any month of the year. Since the 1970s, the population has increased rapidly, which may be a result of the expansion of intensive arable farming and in particular the prevalence of oilseed rape. Most professional pigeon shots shoot them all year round, including in the summer, which is the time when most will be breeding. If the farmer has given you permission to shoot on his land, then that's fine.

According to Will Garfit, the secret of successful wood pigeon shooting is:

'Good reconnaissance. Knowing which field and what time of day; standing in the right place in the field; having a good "hide" which is successful at hiding movement and having effective decoys. You must keep very still until the moment of truth when you get up and shoot. Wood pigeons are very fast at evasive action and even if you get the first bird easily, the second bird will have seen you and be skitting away. You get every shot in the book, and people who shoot wood pigeon tend to be fairly effective on game birds…'

Pigeon hide

8
The Lady Gun

'A woman only knows she's a good shot when the men stop telling her she is…'
Sir Joseph Nickerson

Shooting grounds are literally crawling with lady Guns, especially the ones in the Home Counties, at around 9am after the school run. Over the past ten or fifteen years the various shooting schools have really aimed their marketing at women and it has worked. Shooting instructors report that women learn a lot faster and listen more carefully to instructions than male shots – they really do get very good much more quickly. Those who go on to become competitive clay shots say it's the perfect antidote to the stress of bringing up young children! Lady Guns are no longer so few and far between on the shooting field either these days, which is great for the sport; shooting certainly cannot be accused any more of being a purely male preserve.

However, while it is no longer as extraordinary today as it was in the early 1980s to meet a lady shot on a driven day, it is still not exactly an everyday occurrence and their presence can still cause a bit of a frisson of interest amongst not just the Guns but the shoot staff too. Even now it is unusual to meet a woman who shoots as well as a man. I was at a shoot recently in Sussex and there was another lady Gun shooting which was a novelty for me. We both got the giggles when the shoot host, who was running a very rare commercial day, stood up in the Gun-bus and announced that in the ninety-year history of the shoot they had only ever had one lady Gun shooting there, and certainly never two lady Guns on the same day. He seemed genuinely astounded to have two ladies in the line and I don't think the comment was meant to make us feel particularly welcome!

'...and the cartridge that I would recommend is...'

Respect!

Naturally it goes without saying that you should treat any lady Gun you come across on the shooting field with the utmost respect and consideration. Any misogynistic comments or behaviour will be much frowned upon by your fellow Guns, not to mention the lady Gun herself. As one male Gun observed, in a board-room situation you wouldn't dream of saying to a woman: 'Oh? You're at this meeting with us? How lovely! And you use a pen as well? How long have you been doing that?'

The chances are that if a lady Gun is shooting in the line on a driven bird day, then she will be fairly serious about her shooting, and patronising comments should be avoided. My advice would be: don't single her out and don't draw attention to the fact she is a woman shooting, just treat her as a welcome member of the shooting team.

Speaking as a lady Gun myself and despite having over thirty years shooting experience, I am still prone to nerves before the day starts. The last thing I want is for some fellow Gun to go blundering in, singling me out in front of everyone, asking me questions which he would never dream of asking a male Gun, such as 'So, how much shooting have you done?' My advice to any male Gun would be: try to refrain from expressing surprise or delight at the fact she is shooting with you, and certainly don't enquire if she's using 'a little 20-bore'. For the moment, she just wants to be one of the team, nothing more, nothing less.

Under pressure

If you think you are under pressure on a shoot day as a male Gun, you need to magnify that feeling by about a thousand to understand truly the thoughts of the lone lady Gun as she greets her fellow guests at the start of the day. She knows that unless she shoots straight, behaves impeccably and is every bit as good as the men, she won't somehow be accepted as 'worthy' of acceptance. Shooting has always been such a male-orientated sport that she knows she cannot afford to put a foot wrong. What's worse, if she does make a mistake, it won't go unnoticed. The novice lady shot will feel this all the more acutely.

The fact that the presence of a lady Gun incites a fair degree of curiosity is just one of those things she has to live with. Rather unfairly, everyone, from the fellow Guns, to the beaters, flankers and keepers, will be keeping half an eye on her. Usually this is just out of curiosity, to see if she's safe, or can shoot straight, or if her dog behaves, or whatever it is. If she cocks it up, she will be the talk of the beaters' wagon and you can be sure it will be ten times more noticed by everyone than anything a male shot does. Fortunately all her worries and nerves will usually dissipate if she connects with a few birds during the first drive – most lady Guns relax visibly after this!

Who's who?

The tricky bit for any wannabe-perfect guest is that at the start of the day, it is not easy to distinguish the experienced lady Gun from the novice lady Gun. While the former just wants to be treated like the rest of the team, the latter would no doubt appreciate a little more consideration and reassurance than you would normally offer to a fellow Gun. The problem is, you won't know whether she is a novice shot or not until the day gets under way.

The Townie Chick

Women are safer shots

Lady Guns are on the whole far safer shots than male Guns. They are naturally more cautious and the majority don't have quite the same killing instincts as men. Coupled with the fact that they don't tend to get plastered at lunch, this means that if you have drawn next to a lady Gun, one thing you don't need to fear for is your personal safety. She is far more likely to be a safer shot than you. However, your pride well may come under attack...

As the first drive progresses, I would strongly recommend that you don't poach her birds. If she is a novice shot, this would be unforgivable, as it would be for any novice shot, male or female; if she is a crack shot, it is asking for trouble. Leave a few of those birds that fly right between you both for her. If she dispatches them beautifully, each with a single shot, you know that you don't need to be quite so generous the next time. If you do shoot one of her birds, though, always apologise straightaway, as you would to a male Gun.

Types of lady Gun

There are many different types of lady Gun, but here is an attempt to identify the main three. As you will see, each type needs and deserves different handling. Just to warn you, it will be virtually impossible to work out which category a lady Gun falls into, until the early drives are under way.

1 The Townie Gun-Toting Chick will have recently taken up shooting, encouraged by a doting boyfriend or husband, or perhaps, because she wants to keep an eye on him! She may not be the country type exactly, but she will probably have been very well taught and she may well go for weekly clay-busting lessons. Her lack of experience will only show as a walking Gun or if she has to do snap-shooting in a wood. She probably won't have a crack at a magpie and her marking is unlikely to be up to much either.

2 The Country Keenie will have grown up doing a bit of shooting as a girl, but on the whole she has probably been sent as a beater as her brothers grabbed any spaces in the line. Now older, wiser and probably married to a shoot fanatic, she's taken up shooting properly. Although she has come late to the sport, she will at least know what's expected, so what she lacks in skill is made up for by the fact that she knows the correct form. Given enough shooting opportunities she may well turn into an excellent all-round shot.

3 The Killer Bitch has shot since the age of ten and is every bit as experienced and bloodthirsty as your average male shot, and quite possibly more so. She will tuck into screaming high pigeons while waiting for the drive to start, she will land birds on your head to wake you up or prove a point. She probably shoots two or three times a week. She may well practise clay shooting out of season to keep her eye in and is often to be seen at charity clay days. You patronise the Killer Bitch at your peril...

The Country Keenie

The Killer Bitch

Clothing for the lady shot

Lady shots have never had it so good in terms of shooting clothes. There is a very wide choice as several of the more traditional companies now have a good selection of ladies' wear – such as Holland & Holland and Purdey's. Other suppliers specialise in ladies' shooting clothes, such as The Really Wild Clothing Company, which was launched in 2002 and now has fourteen outlets. It was a very different story twenty years ago, when all the lady shot had available to her was men's jackets in a size small and a very narrow selection of shooting knickerbockers. (A comprehensive list of suppliers will be found in the Appendix at the end of the book.)

If you are starting from scratch, I would recommend an elegant but practical tweed jacket, designed for women, but not too garish a colour, and a couple of pairs of plus fours. Some pretty checked shirts and v-neck sweaters in country colours will complete the picture. For cold days, you should purchase some thin silk polo-necks which will really keep you warm, and some fine woollen tights for under your plus fours. A lightweight waterproof jacket which can be rolled up small and easily carried about, but large enough to cover your tweed jacket, is useful in a downpour. In addition a pair of waterproof trousers is vital for any lady accompanying the Guns, because it means that she can sit anywhere and not worry she will get her trousers wet or muddy. She can peel the waterproofs off at lunchtime and know that her plus fours will be spotless.

Gloves are important for girls as they tend to suffer more than men from cold hands. Hats, of the sort that stay put in a high wind, are also essential for keeping you dry and warm. (I would suggest not too much fur anywhere if you want to look the part in the UK.) A good scarf is practical as it can be wrapped round your ears if the wind really gets up. Silk squares worn as scarves may look attractive to start off with but soon turn very sorry and limp in the rain and don't keep you warm at all.

Lady Guns on lady Guns

Having spoken to many lady Guns about shooting, they all say that the worst thing you might encounter on the field is a mildly patronising attitude. The words you least want to hear are: 'Not a bad shot for a woman!' As my father used to say: 'A woman only knows she's a good shot when the men stop telling her she is.' In my own experience any condescension from male Guns tends to be unintentionally tactless. Once you have shot with them and shown that you are safe and can shoot straight, they usually relax and totally accept you as one of the team.

A fellow lady Gun, Karen Hargreaves, took up shooting around ten years ago. She was once invited on a double gun day. As she only had one gun, she had borrowed a pair from a friend. At the start of the shoot day, before they had drawn numbers, she had a quick practice mounting the borrowed guns to decide whether to use them or just stick with her own gun. At that precise moment her loader for the day appeared. He was clearly horrified at the idea of having to load for a lady. When he saw her practising mounting her gun, he asked: 'Have you shot flying birds before?' Her husband, a very humorous chap replied: 'Oh, they're *flying* birds, no one told us they'd be *flying*!' After the first drive the loader, rather shamefaced, congratulated her, adding: 'Oh, I see you *have* shot flying birds before then…'

Daphne Hanbury, who grew up shooting quail at home in Mississippi, came over to the UK and married a Brit in the 1980s. She is a very handy shot with her 12-bores.

She says:

'I've often been the first girl ever to shoot on an estate, from down in Cornwall to Scotland. It says a lot for the host, they had no hang-ups. But I have had my fair share of other guns really squinting at me, and I could tell they were thinking: "She's either going to kill us or not hit a thing". But if you shoot the first bird of the day, you can relax! The worst thing about being a lady Gun is there often isn't anywhere you can disappear to, there's always a stop or a picker-up hanging around at the start of a drive, and at the end, so many people are wandering around everywhere that you just daren't bare your bottom!'

As you can imagine, it can be very hard for a lady shot to break into shooting properly and be invited to shoot in her own right. The best lady shots tend to be either married to keen shooting men and have their own shooting estate, or have been born into a shooting family and have had access to the sport from a young age. Without these advantages, it is very hard for a woman to rack up the number of driven days required to become a really decent shot.

Ladies' days

Ladies' days are a good way for a lady shot to take part in a driven day without the added pressure of feeling 'different'. I haven't been on many, but my experience of them is that they are immensely confidence boosting, with a non-competitive atmosphere, where everyone is totally charming to each other. If anything everyone holds back rather, not wanting to seem too aggressive! Bill Tyrwhitt-Drake holds an annual ladies' day on his estate at East Meon in Hampshire and has encouraged many women to start shooting in the line, including his wife Philippa, who now shoots regularly. Some estates even use ladies' days as flying practice for the partridges in early September, because the keeper knows that the Guns will shoot carefully and sparingly!

On the whole, very experienced lady shots tend not to flock to ladies' days. The Duchess of Northumberland is renowned as a superb shot; indeed the whole family shoot including her four children, two of whom are daughters.

'I have never been on a ladies' day. Because I've only ever shot on mixed days, I can't really see the point of them. I think it's quite patronising for a shoot owner to say: "We'll have a ladies' day, and husbands will stand behind". I love to have two or three other women in the line, on a normal mixed day. We often shoot the six of us, family, so we make up most of the line, with six badly behaved dogs! There is only room for two guests…'

Frankie Duckworth, who can hold her own against most male shots, grew up in Lancashire and has shot since the age of fifteen, after a real fight to earn the right to start shooting. But she picked it up fast and later spent four years working as a shooting instructor. Frankie is invited everywhere and shoots as much as she can. She says that she shoots badly on ladies' days 'because you have to be so bloody polite! I shoot far better when I've got to be competitive and when I shoot with people who are better than me.'

Men behaving badly…

Jane Northumberland has also occasionally fallen foul of misogynistic behaviour:

'As a lady shot, you have to be able to shoot as well or better than the men… people are watching and waiting to spot the one you missed. I was shooting grouse in Yorkshire once, and I was very lucky, I was in the thick of it, and as Ralph was helping me pick up after the drive, we saw a fellow Gun come up to the butt and start flicking my spent cartridges with his stick into a pile.

'So Ralph took him to one side and asked him what he was doing and he replied: "I've seen the grouse on the top of the butt, and I'm trying to work out the ratio of birds to cartridges". We couldn't believe it!'

Thankfully such incidents are rare and what's far more common is for fellow Guns to greet you like a long-lost friend even though you have no clue who they are. It is so much harder to remember and place someone in context whom you have met once and shot with a few years ago, because seven or eight identikit green- and tweed-clad gents can all somehow merge into one distant memory. Yet you, perhaps the only woman on that shoot, remain etched on their memory.

Despite the plethora of sporting clay shooting courses aimed specifically at women, a lot of lady Guns remain on the clay circuit and don't venture out on to mixed driven days. A combination of lack of opportunity and perhaps the fear of trespassing on what is still a very male preserve keeps them away. In many cases husbands or boyfriends, although happy enough for their wives or girl-friends to buy a gun and go on a clay-shooting course, draw the line at actually sharing a gun with them on a driven day, or – heavens above! – giving up their own peg in the line for them. Buying two pegs in the line is obviously very

'Would you like me to have a go?'

expensive, and a real deterrent for most shooting couples, who tend to share a gun.

I have heard a loathsome remark, made partly in jest, about women on the shooting field, 'Women double the cost and halve the fun'. Doubtless there are those who really believe this to be true. But these days a negative reaction towards women out shooting is positively prehistoric. You do occasionally hear an old fuddy-duddy grumbling into his bull-shot, and one can only assume such men feel threatened in some way. A letter to *The Field*, written as recently as March 2008, expressed the following view:

> 'In these parts it is accepted that birds are best put over the line, not in it. I have heard of isolated incidents but generally people here have concluded that the lady Gun is more effective at cooking game than shooting it and the only positive to come from a ladies' day is that you can squeeze an extra day in at the end of the season.'

I hardly need to add that the correspondent was male.

Perhaps grumbling dinosaurs like him have only encountered the species of lady Gun who let the side down, you know, the Wet and Hopeless kind of lady shot, the kind who needs two men to help her over a fence, who can't carry her own gun and who sits in the vehicle if it's raining. This type doesn't mark or pick her birds, and doesn't think it matters if she doesn't hit a thing all day. As if that wasn't bad enough, she will probably forget to tip the keeper as well. If a man behaved like that, he wouldn't be asked again, but because she is female, she somehow gets away with it. This kind of lady Gun does untold damage to the reputation of all of us, who then rather unfairly get tarred with the same brush.

Mixed teams

On the whole, most Guns would agree that a mixed team makes for a very enjoyable day. David Hicks, an American who has made Britain his home, is a keen shot who takes numerous days up and down the country for himself and his friends:

> 'I always want to put forward the best line I can, firstly in terms of safety, and secondly, socially. If anyone can shoot, is safe and amusing then great. I really enjoy shooting with ladies in the line and lunch is definitely more enjoyable with a few ladies round the table.'

Regarding any specific advice for a lady Gun becoming the perfect guest, I would say that all the advice in this book holds good for both sexes. However, in the box opposite there are a few little pointers specifically aimed at lady shots, gleaned from my own experience, which may be of some use.

Lady Guns – Dos and Don'ts

Shake hands with guests you haven't met before at the start of the day, but feel free to kiss them goodbye at the end of the day (unless they have been truly ghastly to you)

Avoid any garment with too much fur trimming or feathers on it – you don't want to be regarded as a fashion plate

Don't wear too much make-up on shoot days for the same reason

If a neighbouring shot is being greedy or patronising – stand up for yourself

If you are shooting like a drain, don't bang on about it and whatever you do don't cry or walk off

If you are shooting brilliantly, and nobody has said anything, don't brag but compliment your neighbour instead

Don't expect others to run errands for you or carry your gun just because you are a lady shot

If it's pouring with rain and you have forgotten your waterproofs, it's NOT ok to ask if you can remain in the vehicle 'just for this drive'

Remember to take enough cash with you, for the keeper, the sweepstake etc

When looking for a discreet place to have a pee, always check and double-check that you are well hidden – beware pickers-up and stops!

Try to avoid using the downstairs loo at lunch: you will be trespassing on hallowed male ground

Don't kiss the keeper goodbye; a handshake containing his tip is all he's expecting!

9
Loaders

'One of the best things about loading is seeing your Gun shoot well.'
David Maudslay, loader

Many people enjoy having someone to chat to on their peg while waiting for the birds and feel that a loader, even for single gun days, adds hugely to the whole experience. Others would frankly rather be on their own, enjoying the peace and tranquillity of the countryside, with all human distractions restricted to purely in between the drives.

Most of the time out shooting, once you are no longer a novice, you will probably not have a loader unless you shoot with double guns. But just in case you do have one, then you need to know the form.

Whatever your personal preference, sometimes you may have no choice about it. For example your host may not be sure about your level of experience, so you might be given a loader to 'keep you right', and act as a bit of a minder. Don't take offence at this, as it should make you feel more confident and will probably increase your chances too. Your loader will act as a useful second pair of eyes and should also give you the confidence to go for a bird which you might otherwise not have done, fearing it is not yours, or too far, or too high. Often a Gun lacking experience of driven days will miss out on opportunities because he spends so long wondering if it's 'his' bird, or if it's too far, or if it's too dangerous, and then the birds have long gone before he has had time to let off a single shot! While this cautious outlook is to be applauded in one way, it won't help the host fill the bag. Having a 'hole' in the line is not ideal for him, so it's always best to accept the offer of a loader gratefully and make the most of it.

Of course you may receive an invitation to shoot on a double gun day, in which case a loader is obviously vital for changing and reloading your guns. It is important to know what to expect of your loader, and also to understand exactly what his role involves (or doesn't involve).

The role of a loader

Firstly, your loader is not a man-servant. Yes, he'll carry your gun and cartridge bag for you, but he has more in common with a ghillie, a mountain guide or a caddy, so you need to treat him with respect. If you are an able-bodied man, and especially if your loader is getting on in years, it would be kind to offer to help him and carry one of the guns up the hill if you are grouse shooting.

He will probably know the estate quite well, he will know where the birds might break cover, he will be a second pair of eyes for spotting birds, and he may, if he's a shooting man himself (which many of them are), be able to help you if you are not swinging through fast enough, or doing something else wrong which will hinder your chances. When grouse shooting, he will almost always have a pair of sticks to place on either side of the top of the butt so that you can shoot more safely, but it is up to you to help decide exactly where to place them so that they are exactly in line with the neighbouring Guns.

Multi-talented loaders

Some of the more experienced loaders are rather multi-talented and can somehow manage, as well as loading fast and furiously, to keep count of how many birds you shoot each drive and mark them too. But you mustn't take this for granted, because your loader may miss seeing where the birds land when he's reloading quickly. After the drive, a good loader will sleeve up the guns, put them somewhere where they won't be trodden on or driven over (yes, that can happen!) and then help you pick up your birds. Some loaders will bring their dogs and if you would rather work your own dog, just explain that you'd like to give yours a chance first. A good loader will be respectful of your wishes and only work his dog when needed.

Chatting on the peg?

A good loader soon gets a sense of whether the Gun likes to chat while waiting for the birds to come, or would rather stay silent. Ideally he should follow your lead and let you be the one to initiate conversation. Some Guns hate any chatting on the peg but not all loaders have learned to gauge this, keeping up a stream of banter all drive long which can be off-putting for your concentration. If you suddenly become unresponsive, your loader should get the hint. But don't be afraid to initiate a conversation, as it will make the day far more pleasant for both of you if you do have the occasional chat, and you may stand to learn a great deal about the estate, the shoot and the local area.

In the north, particularly on grouse moors, your loader might well be a local keeper, a farmer, a dairyman or a shepherd. Preference is often given to local farming tenants to act as loaders or flankers which is good for the ongoing relationship between the shoot and its tenants. A team of Guns who have leased a day on the moors and who each turn up with their own loader from elsewhere doesn't always go down very well with the locals.

There's no knowing quite what profession your loader may have: I have met firemen, policemen, miners, paramedics and also accountants, lawyers, electricians and doctors! If you don't chat to your loader, then you will miss a great opportunity, as they are often fascinating people. If you are worried that the chat will distract you, you can always stop as soon as the birds start coming over, and your loader will soon be too busy changing guns to manage much of a conversation.

Above all, be polite and treat your loader with respect, and certainly don't blame him for your lack of shooting prowess! The ultimate compliment is if you return somewhere to shoot the following season and your loader has asked the keeper if he can load for you again.

Loaders love loading

Loaders mostly go loading for the love of it; they enjoy meeting new people, they enjoy being out in the countryside and being part of a shoot day. They usually derive great pleasure if their Gun shoots well and appreciates their help. The 'tip' they receive at the end of the day, for lugging your gear around in all weathers, and looking after you, is certainly not the only reason that they are there.

Roy Burrows is a full-time keeper at Barningham, a grouse moor and pheasant shoot in North Yorkshire, but he goes loading at neighbouring estates because local keepers tend to help each other out in this way. He has loaded, as he puts it, 'for kings, princes and paupers'! A very accurate shot himself, he has an amazing talent for being extremely good company, yet has sharp eyes for spotting the birds early on, loads incredibly quickly and marks what you kill accurately. He also doubles up as a bit of a shooting coach and will tell you after each bird is missed why you missed it, and what to do with the next one. If you follow his advice, you do ultimately kill more grouse. Needless to say, he is in high demand as a loader.

Roy explains why he likes going loading:

'I enjoy the day, I like the social side, meeting different people. My ideal Gun? A good shot, good company… It makes my day a lot better if you get on with them, as you are spending a lot of time just the two of you waiting for the birds. Some I wouldn't like to load for again... the ones who treat you like an inferior being, like a servant. But mostly I've ended up learning a lot of things, striking up

'…and what's your wife's hobby?'

new friendships. I finished up going skiing with one person I loaded for and another I keep in touch with all the time, although I only loaded for him once.'

One of the more difficult things Roy has had to do is to tell a member of a European royal family that he was shooting dangerously. Ultimately the loader is not responsible for the actions of the Gun but as Roy said 'if you see something dangerous, you've got to try and stop it'.

Striking gold

If your loader is amusing, entertaining and friendly as well as being a great loader, then you have struck gold. Finding a good loader is a bit like finding a new partner: you may not strike it lucky the first time, but don't let that put you off the whole experience! Once you find a good one, if he's from your local area, it is worth getting his number, so that you can ask him to load for you again on those occasions when you need one.

Just as top golfers attribute some of their success to their caddies, and stalkers come to rely on a particular ghillie, Guns can come to absolutely depend on a particular loader. You become an inseparable 'team'. Often loaders will act as shooting coaches, and clay ground instructors are sometimes asked to accompany the Guns to shoots for this purpose.

I have often thought that the job of a loader is not dissimilar to that of a top-notch nanny. This is especially true of a career loader, someone who may well be retained by a Gun all year round to be responsible for all the kit and the general welfare of their employer. They frequently double up as drivers too. A good loader will encourage his Gun if he is not doing well or congratulate him on a good day. Very good ones will even anticipate the Gun's needs before he has had a chance to articulate them. They are one step ahead, and put the Gun's needs first at all times. It's not uncommon for a close bond to form between a Gun and his loader.

Joe Woodcock, for example, is one of the fastest loaders in the land. Utterly professional and discreet, he loads for Robert Miller whenever he shoots both at Gunnerside and elsewhere, a job he has been doing for six or seven years now. Joe describes the perfect loader:

'He should try and help the Gun he is loading for by telling him about the direction the birds may be coming from and which is the shortest sky line for them. He should be quick, should make sure the others Guns are safe, should place the sticks in the right place, spot the birds, look after all the kit. If any Gun swings the gun even a little bit dangerously, he should stamp on it straight away and if he does it again, he should report him to the owner or keeper.'

Joe also has strong views on how the perfect Gun should behave; he hates arrogance. 'He should never say things like "quick, quick, quick": you are there to make his day better but you are not his servant.'

David Maudslay, who works for the Environment Agency, lives in Holme upon Spalding Moor, a rural village between York and Hull. He will often travel 150 miles in a day to go loading up in the Yorkshire Dales.

> 'I've been going loading for about ten years. Normally I'll do about twenty days in a year. I love the wildness of it, especially up in the Dales. I enjoy working as a team: especially if your Gun is shooting well and the changeovers are smooth. I also enjoy picking up with my dogs. One of the best things about loading is seeing your Gun shoot well.

> 'I find it easier to load double guns, because when you are just stuffing and the Gun is opening the gun, you are reliant on angles, and them facing the right way, and not shutting any fingers in. Problems can start when a Gun not used to double-gunning starts breaking the gun before he hands it to me. Clonking the barrels is another big no-no.'

Willie Peel can think of no better loader than his head grouse keeper at Grinton, North Yorkshire. Desmond Coates is known throughout the dales for his practical jokes and his in-depth knowledge of grouse and their ways. Prior to Coates, Peel enjoyed a long loading relationship with Robert John Guy, who was his loader for twenty-five years at Gunnerside. 'He is still alive, living in Richmond, I go and see him every two or three months. I love him dearly, we have a very special relationship.'

Up to mischief

Desmond Coates enjoys loading for James Percy when he comes to shoot in the Yorkshire Dales. As a rule, James is not a competitive shot, but one year when shooting at Arkengarthdale in a bumper year, he and some fellow guests placed a bet as to who would shoot the most grouse the next day. Desmond got to hear about this and decided to play a trick on James. The morning of the shoot, he arrived clutching a bandaged right hand, complete with splodges of blood. He said he'd been out fox lamping the night before and caught it on the Argocat. James was naturally concerned for Desmond, who appeared to be putting on a brave face.

Knowing what a handicap to his shooting Desmond's injured hand would be, James discreetly tried to ascertain if any other loader was available. All the other Guns were in on the joke including his host who told him most definitely that no one else was available and that he couldn't just shoot with a single gun either. Once at their butt, Desmond suggested they have a bit of a practice. He was slow and clumsy, dropping cartridges all over the place. James had his head in his hands on the side of the butt. About ten minutes into the drive, Desmond suddenly whipped off the bandage saying he'd been miraculously healed! James was so furious he chased

Desmond all the way down the moor, kicking his backside as they went.

Bobby McAlpine, who runs high pheasant shoot Llanarmon in North Wales, is in much demand as a shooting guest all over the country. He explains why he always has a loader.

'I hate loading for myself. I am not good at carrying all the equipment – guns, cartridges, shooting stick etc. I am also very slow at putting the cartridges in, and have got totally used to a loader doing it for me. Of course with two guns a loader is essential anyway. I also like to be driven after a shoot as I enjoy having a drink or two at lunch and possibly after shooting. I am lucky to have had only the two excellent loaders during my shooting lifetime. Basil Davies, who loaded for me for thirty years was a great character. My current loader, Bob Messer, was a policeman for thirty-five years and has loaded for me for years. Whereas Basil could hardly see out of the butt, Bob is very good at spotting grouse coming. I have tried to get him to say right, left, centre but he finds this very difficult and usually thumps me on the shoulder instead!'

On meeting your loader

Always make sure you get his name, and if you forget it before the first drive, just ask him again. (This is less embarrassing on the first drive than it is on the last!) Your loader may take your gun and cartridge bag from you when you meet. Once you have drawn for numbers, tell him what yours is and he will have a good idea which part of the line to head towards.

On the peg

Once on the peg, if you are using two guns, you could help by un-sleeving one of the guns yourself, whilst your loader gets the other one ready. If you have not had this loader before, or you are not that familiar with shooting with two guns, it's as well to have a quick practice so that you can work out where you are both going to stand. Some loaders will have a strong grip and literally push the gun at you, half knocking you over, whereas others will hold it rather limply and hand it to you more delicately, whereupon you are more likely to drop it or clash barrels. Somewhere in between is good.

It goes without saying that when you are practising, do so with empty barrels. When you are ready to start shooting, you should always look down the barrels before putting in the cartridges: it is your responsibility to check for any blockages. Some Guns insist on always putting in the first two cartridges themselves.

During the drive

If you fire just one shot, it's good practice always to change guns, so you then have two barrels if another bird flies over. Some loaders are so keen for you to change that I have known them try to grab the gun out of my hands if I dither too long about whether to take another shot with the remaining barrel or not! Always remember to slide the safety catch on as you hand the gun over, to save an accidental firing if the loader mistakenly pulls the trigger while changing the guns. Toggles or buttons on clothing can be quite dangerous in this way. An accidental discharge at such close range would result in very serious damage and you often hear people say that the person most likely to kill you when you are shooting, is in fact your loader. During the drive, try to keep a regular count of how many birds you have down, and check with your loader from time to time to make sure you both know where the birds have fallen.

At the end of the drive

Sleeve up the gun you are holding, let your loader sleeve up the other, and then set off to find the birds. Some loaders like to tidy the cartridges first into a neat pile and some even count them so they can keep a note of your cartridge-to-bird ratio! Personally I prefer them not to do this…

A good loader should really try to help you find your birds. Even if he hasn't got a dog, he should set forth with you in an attempt to find them, or hail a picker-up to help you. It's very much a team effort. A loader who strides off to the vehicles straight after the drive to chat with his mates, has only done half his job, in my opinion – unless of course, there was just nothing to pick!

At the end of the day

Your loader may well offer to clean your gun, and you could find him your cleaning kit unless there is one he can use elsewhere, perhaps if there is a communal gun-room. Remember, it's not done to disappear inside for your delicious hot crumpets and cake and leave your loader waiting for ages for his tip. He will probably be in a hurry to get away and it's not fair to delay him as he won't be able to leave until he has handed back the guns. Try and sort all this out before you go in for tea and deal with the tipping quickly and without fuss. Your host or shoot organiser will guide you as to the correct amount and it is always worth checking each year.

If the terrain has been very difficult, or it has been inclement weather, or if your loader has been a terrific help marking and picking up the birds, you can err on the side of generosity and give him a bit more. With rising fuel costs, you should also bear in mind how far he's had to travel. As you thank him and tell him how much you have appreciated his help, hold out your hand to shake his and transfer the correct amount into his hand without drawing attention to it. Some Guns just tuck the notes in one of their loader's pockets. Sometimes loaders feel rather awkward about being tipped, and some have told me they would far prefer to just pick up a wage packet at the end of the day like the beaters and flankers. However, shooting is an archaic institution in many ways and so it is unlikely that this ancient tradition will change.

Getting it very wrong

A Northern Irish friend of mine, after his first day shooting grouse, got into a bit of a muddle when the time came to tip his loader, a local sheep farmer. My friend did the usual handshake/tip and later, when it was time to tip the keeper, he looked appalled and came running up to me, ashen-faced, hissing: 'I've given him the wrong wad of notes! I mixed up which wad was for the keeper! What do I do now?'

I was no help at all. I had no extra cash to lend him that day and naturally, keepers don't take cheques or credit cards. I couldn't stop giggling as he really was in a very agitated state. There was quite a difference in the amount, as he was tipping the keeper for two days and the loader for one. In the end, he had no choice but to go back to his loader and sheepishly ask for the wad back. He then proceeded to try to remove a few of the £20 notes while his loader looked on appalled... I was just so glad it wasn't me.

10
The Shoot Lunch

'A shooting day is nothing without a decent lunch'
Peter Holt, author of *The Keen Shot's Miscellany*

Any Brit who goes shooting abroad, especially if he is keen on his food, will probably be very shocked by the sparsity of the lunch on offer. Even at the grandest of shoots, with huge schlosses, lakes and follies, whose owners have more titles than easily fit on to their headed notepaper, all you get is a plain sausage or some cured ham and a slice of bread. Any kind of soup is a bonus. It really is, in the words of an Austrian friend of mine, 'peasant food'. Shoot lunches outside Britain just do not tend to reflect adequately the grandeur of the surroundings or the quality of the sport. Of course this frugal fare is arguably far better for your waistline but that's not the point.

In Britain we like to make a big thing about our shooting lunches. In Peter Holt's book, *The Keen Shot's Miscellany*, he includes an excerpt from the Victorian shooting writer, J. J. Manley, who in 1902 observes:

'It is an utter mistake to imagine that cold viands are most appropriate for heated and jaded frames... As to your drink, that is an entirely different matter. Let that be as cold as possible... Do not be in a hurry with your lunch, nor afterwards. Take a cigar, lie on your back, stretch your legs, with your heels up if possible, after the sensible American fashion. Even a siesta – a short one of course – in my opinion is not only allowable but advisable in some cases. A full hour or an hour and a half devoted to luncheon is not time lost, to say nothing of the agreeable way of spending it.'

Food glorious food

There are some exceptions to the poor grub on offer outside Britain and in Spain it's a different story. Food plays a huge part in the proceedings, and not just at lunch, but in between drives too! So often you will hear, when you ask a friend how they got on when they come back from shooting in Spain, 'Ooh! The lunches are fantastic, you sit out in a field, and they cook you paella' or 'The tapas were amazing'. This information always seems to come before any description of the quality of the birds, which shows you just how important shooting lunches are to us Brits.

Lunches are a big thing…

Shoot lunches in this country are usually very festive occasions (but hopefully not too festive on the alcohol front, about which more later) and finding a good 'lunch lady' is often a top priority for a shoot host. At a typical, traditional British shoot lunch, you will often sit down to a three-course meal plus cheese, coffee and biscuits. Quite often you will have to consume all this in under an hour! Maggie Wyvill, who hosts wonderful shoot days, often six days a week, from her beautiful Yorkshire home says:

> 'On pheasant days, the lunches have to be quick, nourishing and nursery, hence we never offer a first course. Cheese, celery and fruit cake come in at the same time as the pudding, so people can either choose or have both quickly. A useful tip is always to serve sloe gin with the cheese and coffee.'

Some of the country's keenest shots will shoot six days out of seven, and their girths really do expand substantially by the time the season is in full swing. Unlike the rest of the country who start their diets on 1 January, shooting folk start theirs on 2 February! Shooting and dieting just don't mix. We should probably blame this on the Edwardians, who held lavish shooting house parties, shot obscene numbers of birds and ate obscene amounts of food. The darling of them all was the then Prince of Wales, reputed gourmet and famed sportsman. Ever since that era, food and shooting have gone hand in hand.

Lunch locations

Shoot lunches are held in all sorts of places: in pubs, in old shepherds' huts on the moor, in specially built wooden lunch huts, in grand ancestral dining rooms, al fresco, in cricket pavilions. By far the most beautiful of all the places I have had lunch in was an octagonal Victorian shooting lodge in the middle of a fir wood in Lincolnshire, which was incredibly romantic. By contrast, John Apthorpe, who is a great shot and bon viveur, has had an articulated lorry converted into a special shoot lunch-room, complete with kitchen and paintings on the wall, which is very luxurious and practical, as it can be taken wherever it is needed.

One of the oddest places I have had a shooting lunch was as the guest of a friend who had taken a day at Powis Castle in Wales, which is open to the public. The car

The shoot lunch

park was rather busy and we decided, sensibly, to bring our guns inside. We walked into the lunch venue, gun sleeves on shoulders, to find the shoot lunch was in fact taking place in the National Trust cafeteria. The scene was rather surreal, with everyone staring or glaring at us as we self-consciously made our way to one corner where our table was laid up. We stood our weapons in the corner under the watchful eyes of several rather nervous tourists.

Bring your own?

At some shoots, it is still absolutely the norm to be asked to bring your own lunch… Rough shoots, or small family shoots, don't make a big deal of lunch. Some perfectly good shoots don't ever provide a hot lunch, regardless of Siberian temperatures outside, or keep things very simple, offering just a baked potato and a sausage, or cold ham and bread. But increasingly it has become the norm – no doubt driven by the demands of corporate let days – for the lunch to be a bit more substantial and well, *special*. On certain shoots there has definitely been a return to the days of Edwardian gluttony, where getting up from the groaning table to take on the elements and do the birds justice becomes very hard indeed… The days of being offered only light beer or cider at lunch with no wine and certainly no champagne are far fewer than they used to be in the early 1980s. These days, Guns have all got rather used to being offered a full range of pre-lunch drinks, quite often champagne or spirits, and then red and white wine with the lunch followed by various liqueurs afterwards, especially sloe gin or port.

Top choices

Popular shoot menus usually feature a soup to start with and then a hearty beef stew or roast beef, or cottage pie. This would be followed by an old-fashioned pudding and then cheese and biscuits. Sarah Lofthouse, keeper's wife and 'lunch lady' par excellence, who caters about four lunches every week of the season starting on 12 August, says:

> 'The menu that goes down the best in cold weather is tomato soup, beef bourguignon and sticky toffee pudding… They all love it and ask for it every time. My worst nightmare was when a vegan was part of the team. There was absolutely nothing I could offer him apart from bread and sliced tomato, as even the vegetable soup had chicken stock in it…'

Who has ever heard of a shooting vegan?

Two kinds of shoot lunch

There are two kinds of shoot lunch. You may stop at around 1pm and have around one hour for lunch, and then have more drives afterwards. Otherwise you 'shoot through', stopping for a late lunch at around 3pm, after shooting has finished. Both options are popular for different reasons, but on the whole it's fair to say that beaters and pickers-up prefer to 'shoot through' – they can get home in good time to tend to their other tasks and don't have to sit there twiddling their thumbs for an hour or so while you have your lunch.

Stopping for lunch after three or four drives is perhaps more traditional. It means that any non-shooting guests can arrive to join the Guns and it makes for a more social event. It also puts a time limit on the lunch – on days where you've 'shot through' you can finish at seven or eight o'clock at night and sometimes much later!

The benefits of stopping halfway through the day are all the more appreciated if the weather is appalling; quite literally you get a respite from the elements and can boost your blood sugar levels before embarking on more drives in the afternoon.

Shooting through offers the lady Gun absolutely no solution to the enduring problem of having to bare her bottom in public when she needs a pee. At least if you stop for lunch, unless it's in a barn or you're halfway up the moor, you are assured of a proper loo. All morning you may not have had the chance for what the Americans call 'a comfort break' because it is near impossible to elude the eagle eyes of around thirty men – beaters, flankers, pickers-up and stops – who seem to lurk around every corner.

Nowhere is it trickier to find a convenient place to disappear to for a quick pee than on a grouse moor. Lady shots should make do with a brief trip behind a stone wall or bobbing down in the bracken because at lunch you may find yourself in trouble. Unless you go before lunch, when you arrive at some old stone hut, or worse,

by a babbling brook, you will have to sit with crossed legs barely drinking a thing lest it contribute any more to the discomfort you are enduring! Some grouse moor owners have been particularly thoughtful and provide a special little wooden hut with a camping loo inside, behind or next to the lunch hut, especially for us ladies. Each of Bob Miller's many lunch huts on his moor, Gunnerside, has one of these, a godsend for the lady shot. It seems he had no choice really, as his three daughters apparently insisted. I don't blame them.

Getting back to food – on the whole, eating and drinking form a major part of any shoot day. Often one has a cooked breakfast first thing and after a couple of drives (but not usually on grouse moors, oddly enough) there is a mid-morning snack which can be substantial and involve sausages or sausage rolls, bread sticks, crisps and biscuits as well as soup, coffee, sloe gin or 'sloe-gasm' which is a mix of champagne and sloe gin. A short time later, or so it seems, and it's time for lunch!

Seek out your host

This is the time when everyone is feeling exhilarated by the morning's sport, your fellow Guns are far more chatty and friendly than they were at the start of the day, and everyone has something to talk about, usually centring on the shooting of course. If you haven't already had the chance to chat to your host and tell him what a wonderful day you are having (which the perfect guest should really have already done by now) the shoot lunch is THE time to seek him out and tell him. As well as thanking him, it's a good idea to comment on anything that has particularly struck you, such as a certain drive where the birds flew particularly well, or the efficiency of the beaters, or a picker-up who was especially helpful, or how fast your loader is, or whatever it may be.

Hosts and shoot organisers and keepers, in fact everyone associated with organising the day, will always be pleased to hear sincere praise about it. Put yourself in your host's shoes for a moment: he will feel much better about the day if he knows that his guests are really enjoying themselves.

Alternatively, if things have gone badly, and you sense your host is anxious, you could go over and be sympathetic, lending a listening ear to his grumbles about what has gone wrong but insisting that you and everyone else are still enjoying the day. Reassure him if the bag isn't what it should be, tell him the conditions are against you, that the keeper is doing his best to present the birds, it's just that the Guns can't hit them!

Lunchtime rituals

A 'sweep' may well take place during lunch, either in the form of guessing the total birds shot, or sometimes the number of shots fired, or the number of different species

'It's the only way of getting the guns out again after lunch.'

shot. You will usually be asked to put in a tenner, or perhaps £20, and the winner often donates half the proceeds to an organisation such as the Countryside Alliance, or the Game and Wildlife Conservancy Trust. It is always a good idea to take part in these sweeps but don't put too low a number down or your host may be insulted!

Don't dawdle

Once lunch is over, and sometimes even before you have finished if time is short, your shoot host will announce that you have only five minutes left… Do not ignore this, as the chances are he will leave the table immediately and start gathering his stuff together and you will be late. Also, by setting an example to your fellow Guns perhaps your host won't have to peel them away from their plates. Thank the lunch lady or chef and slip them a note if it seems appropriate.

Any last minute kit changes or finding more cartridges must be done right away. Wandering about in a drunken haze saying protracted goodbyes in your socks to each and every lunch guest while everyone else waits for you in their vehicles is just not on. The beaters will have blanked in, the birds will be edgy, and you need to be absolutely ready on time.

Shooting through

In the late 1970s and early 1980s the trend to shoot through began in earnest. It tends to be favoured by teams shooting late in December and in January when the light fades fast, as well as by those who don't want to have to limit their alcohol intake at lunch. Keepers' days and rough shoots often shoot through so that everyone can be home at a reasonable time.

A keeper comments:

'In winter I much prefer to shoot through. Sometimes if it's absolutely hammering down with rain, I really cringe when I have to tell the beaters they've got to sit and wait for an hour and a half while the Guns have their lunch. We might only need another fifty birds. One day, it was that bad, that three-quarters of the beaters went home! When the owner came out after lunch and I told him they'd gone, he was furious and said: "But we are paying them for a full day!" But for £25 a day, you just can't do that to people.'

Alcohol and the shoot lunch

One advantage of shooting through is that you can indulge in a pre-lunch gin and tonic and enjoy whatever wine is on offer at lunch without the worry that you might accidentally shoot dangerously under the influence of alcohol. I doubt any judge or jury would look favourably on a Gun who accidentally shot someone while plastered. As Sir Anthony Milbank says: 'You could imagine yourself in court and the prosecution saying:

"Now tell me what happened, you had a shotgun in your hand, with two cartridges, and *how much* alcohol did you have to drink? So you leave the lunch, pick up your shotgun and proceed to shoot someone…" No, it doesn't sound good!'

At least shooting through means that you can relax totally, knowing the day is over and the party can begin. I've heard of many shooting 'lunches' that didn't end until 10 or 11pm! Some Guns have drivers to take them home which is sensible given the amount of alcohol consumed… But it's a very long day for them because they have usually been loading all day too.

Don't overdo it

From start to finish, your whole day out shooting will be peppered with offers of alcoholic drinks. First sloe gin may be passed around when you all gather at the start of the shoot, perhaps poured into numbered shot glasses which could be the way your host chooses to draw for numbers. Then at elevenses there is more sloe gin, at lunch there are pre-lunch drinks, followed by wine and more sloe gin and possibly port afterwards. Later at tea it's entirely possible that a glass of whisky could be pressed into your hand along with your cup of tea. There's certainly a lot of alcohol on offer out shooting but whatever you do, never get drunk or you may well jeopardise your chances of being asked again.

Someone told me a story about a guest getting on in years who at a shoot lunch poured himself what he thought were a couple of 'virgin Marys' (non-alcoholic) from a jug, not realising that they were in fact full-on Bloody Marys. After some wine with lunch and a glass or two of port, he found at the end of the meal that he simply couldn't stand up… A chief constable who was also shooting decided to send the gentleman home.

Mike Barnes tells another story:

'I have been on a shoot where after a day in which we had done the odd bit of shooting between drinks, the host had fallen fast asleep on the pub floor. On waking, he rounded up his team of Guns to take on the hapless birds occupying the dovecote in his nearby garden. The dovecote was quite ancient and a some-what grand affair so some of the shooting was almost sporting – though not necessarily safe! Thankfully our host faded quite quickly and before long was horizontal again on the pub floor. By now it was early evening and customers were stepping over him to order their drinks.'

As Jonathan Irby sensibly advises:

'It's at the host's discretion, but a good shoot host should not ply his guests with too much alcohol and good guests should not drink too much. My personal philosophy is to have one glass of wine on a shoot day, no more than if you want to drive. If you shouldn't operate a car with more than a certain intake, you shouldn't wield a gun either. I always tell novice shots going on their first game day to drink as if they were going to drive.'

Banning alcohol!

I discovered recently that in the Czech Republic, which has some superb pheasant shooting, all alcohol consumption on shoot days has been made illegal. It's the only European country where this is the case but I can't help wondering if this zero-tolerance approach will spread further afield.

A lucky escape

A few seasons ago, a chap was driving down the A1 still in his shooting clothes after an excellent day's shooting, but he was going at over 100mph and he got pulled over by the police. He thinks: 'Oh no, here we go, my shotgun licence will be taken away, I'll be breathalysed, done for speeding…' When the officer asks him to step out of the vehicle and sees his plus fours he asks: 'Did you have a good day, sir?' He asked where he had been shooting and it turned out the officer knew the place well, he liked picking-up there and did a bit of shooting himself. They chatted about the day for a few minutes and the Gun was sent on his way. Not all stories involving policemen and guns are quite so cheery!

Brewing up trouble

A group of Guns was accused by a local man of killing a bird of prey on a shoot day. The police arrived, the shoot was disrupted, and a great long discussion ensued, after which it became clear that they had done no such thing. The local was an 'anti' trying to stir up trouble for them. But a policeman had smelled alcohol on the breath of some the Guns and he not only took their guns away, but also the driving licences of those with cars. It put a bit of a dampener on the day to say the least.

Them and us?

A final observation on shoot lunches: the Guns eating lunch in a separate location to the shoot staff is perfectly normal. A stranger to shooting might think that this is completely inappropriate in today's world. I can't really explain why it is like it is, except to say that shooting is very traditional and tends to follow set rules which were laid down hundreds of years ago. It would have been unthinkable then to eat lunch with your keeper and the beaters. Some shoots now do pride themselves on mixing Guns with shoot staff at lunch while others wouldn't dream of it. I have done both and both are just as enjoyable, but in totally different ways. New shoots often do have a system where the whole shooting party, including beaters, pickers-up and flankers all join together, usually in a large barn, and share lunch.

A friend who recently relocated to Somerset says:

'We never did this before, but when we moved to Somerset, the tradition on our shoot seemed to be for everyone to eat together at long tables in the barn. There are about forty or fifty of us, Guns, beaters, keepers and pickers-up. Friends I invite to shoot sometimes ask me why this is, but the truth is, there is no reason not to! It's how it has always been here, and it would just seem odd to segregate everyone from the Guns. It makes for a really fun atmosphere.'

Shoot Lunch Dos and Don'ts

Remove your boots – wear shoes or just your socks

Always take your gun inside and leave your dog outside

Don't hog the loo

Protect dining chairs from wet bottoms if your trousers are muddy or damp

Go and chat to your host: show your gratitude

Don't be a shoot bore to non-shooting lunch guests

Go easy with the alcohol on offer

Be ready to leave on time for the afternoon drives

Remember to thank everyone for lunch: don't just walk off

11
Parting Shots

'The tip should reflect the difficulty of producing sport on the day. Always ask your host but if you are uncertain, err on the generous side.'
Mark Firth of the Countryside Alliance

At the end of a wonderful day's shooting, one of the most important things you must do is to tip the keeper. This is a tradition which harks back to the age when keepers were paid virtually nothing and tips really did form a huge chunk of their salaries. Things have changed of course and the majority of keepers, at least on the larger estates, earn a decent wage. Don't forget, though, that they regularly work twelve hours a day, or in the rearing season, up to eighteen hours a day, seven days a week. Compared to your average desk-bound office worker, who may work thirty-five or forty hours in a week, a keeper's salary still doesn't seem to reflect adequately the amount of hours worked and the sheer effort put in. You could argue that keepers are often provided with a house, a car, and other living expenses, but no keeper does his job for the money. It really is a vocation, a way of life. It can be one of the loneliest of jobs, and statistically has a high suicide rate.

If keepers were paid by the hour, they would be taking home a huge salary. But as none of them do count their hours, then the tip really does help to compensate them for all the hard grind and extra hours. Most Sundays a keeper will be out and about, and their day starts very early in the rearing season, at first light. On shoot days, in the main on Saturdays, their day might start at 6am and won't finish till well past 7pm or later. In the days running up to a shoot day, they will spend many an evening on the phone organising beaters, flankers, and pickers-up.

How much to tip?

There are various theories regarding the correct amount to tip, such as '£20 per hundred birds shot, per Gun', but this formula isn't always foolproof. My father used to say that it was not just the keeper's work that day which had given you sport, but, on a well-run shoot, 'unremitting effort the whole year round'.

Mark Firth of the Countryside Alliance agrees:

'Always ask your host, if you are uncertain, but err on the generous side. I get cross with any institutionalised formula for tipping keepers, because there is a massive difference on estates where 500-bird days happen three times a week, and other shoots where to get 200 birds on a really tricky day is really good.'

If there are any under-keepers, the tip will usually be divided between them, so you may also want to take account of the number of under-keepers when you work out how much to tip.

Generally speaking tips can range from£20 to £40 per head for a 250-bird day pheasant shooting but can be much more for wild partridge and grouse, to reflect the difficulties of keepering and showing wild birds.

If you have had a particularly good drive, or you feel it has been one of the best day's sport ever, then add another tenner. You can be sure it will be appreciated.

Guide the others

If you are a regular on a shoot and you know that a guest is new to the place, it's a kindness to take him to one side and point him in the right direction regarding the correct amount to tip. This is so he doesn't have to bother the host or feel unsure. If no one is sure what the form is, then one Gun should ask the host and just pass the information round the others, which saves a lot of hassle.

How to tip

One shooting guest was in very bad odour when he tipped the keeper whilst talking on his mobile phone. The next time, the same man got his driver to tip the keeper. This is obviously the height of bad manners.

When you go to tip the keeper, firstly, make sure you have the right man, and don't accidentally go to the shoot organiser instead. That is not to say that you shouldn't thank everyone involved, especially the under-keepers. Not enough people do this, so be sure to thank them and shake their hands too. But when you are ready to thank the head keeper, your previously counted-out wad of folded notes will be discreetly concealed in the palm of your right hand. As you shake his hand and thank him, the notes will be swiftly and easily transferred as you take your hand away.

Apparently there is one keeper who has an eight-pocket waistcoat so he always

Eight pockets for eight tips

knows who has under-tipped him! The keeper will be sure to report this to his host. It really is one of the most heinous crimes you can commit out shooting – apart from shooting someone! As Mark Firth says 'If people ask me: "Which one is the keeper?" I say to them, try and leave without tipping him and you'll soon find out!'

One keeper in Yorkshire tells me that finding he has been tipped in US dollars or euros is quite common. 'It is annoying, but I just save them for when I go on holiday!'

The keeper at Orelton in Shropshire told me that a disgruntled Gun once tipped him saying: 'And here's another tenner so you can get yourself a dog lead', because the keeper's dog had on a couple of occasions caused a lot of birds to flush at once.

A bachelor friend of ours once went to thank the keeper and started telling him chummily about one of the pickers-up he'd found very attractive and that he'd been chatting her up between drives all day. He was busy extolling her virtues with a lot of nudge-nudge wink-wink, when the keeper remarked sourly: 'Eh, well, I'll tell my daughter you liked her...'

How to be Asked Again

The brace of birds

After tipping the keeper, you will usually be handed a brace of birds. It is best not to refuse these, even though it might be a case of taking coals to Newcastle. Even though your partner (or butcher!) might not be enthusiastic about the prospect of having yet more birds to pluck, even though your deep freeze is still bursting with last year's birds, you really should accept them gracefully. It just gives shooting a bad name if birds are not taken – there must be someone you know who might like them even if you don't want them yourself.

The Game-to-Eat campaign, now in its ninth year, has done a lot to increase awareness and enjoyment of British game. Their spokesperson says:

> 'Game is wild, natural and free range and if you're looking for something low in fat and cholesterol, game is a delicious and healthy alternative to many other red meats. Pheasant and partridge also contain a high level of iron, protein, vitamin B (6) and selenium, which helps to protect cells from damage caused by free radicals.'

A large pheasant will easily feed a family of four. Our children were brought up eating pheasant, even though when they were younger we called it chicken for a while to get them used to it. Out of the game season, I am unpopular if I buy a chicken to roast if a pheasant still lurks in our freezer from the previous season.

I once made the mistake of pressing a brace of birds on the wife of a novice Gun who'd refused to take them. She looked very dubious but I ranted on about a good local butcher in Fulham who would pluck them for a fiver, and muttered a quick recipe to her. She held them gingerly and I thought to myself (with some degree of self-satisfaction) that I had helped to introduce someone to the delights of eating game. Speaking to her some weeks later, I enquired whether she had enjoyed the pheasants. She blushed and, very embarrassed, she admitted that she had not had the heart to eat them; they had remained strung up on a tree in her garden for three weeks until eventually the family decided to hold a burial service in their garden in Wandsworth as she couldn't bear to throw such beautiful birds in the dustbin. Clearly some people are not convinced as to the benefits of eating game!

Going home

If you have to stop en route for petrol on your way home from the shoot, you may well get funny looks from people on the garage forecourt if you stride about in your plus fours. It's not a bad idea to have a pair of jeans to change into after shooting if you are driving long distances.

When you get home

After a day's shooting there is always so much to be done: obviously you need to

154

unload the car, feed the dog, clean the gun, lock it away safely, write up your game book if you keep one, and then your very next task should be to write the thank you letter…In reality you fall into a bath, have a lovely soak, eat some dinner and collapse into bed. Several days may go by before you sit down to write your letter and in some cases it might be several weeks, or months, or perhaps never!

With ever escalating costs, a shooting invitation is a very special present indeed. Regardless of how much shooting your host may have at his disposal, it is still a great honour to have been included. The very least you can do as a guest is to write a decent thank-you letter. Piffa Schroder agrees: 'You should *always* write your thank-you letter so that it catches the next day's post – manners apart, it makes an indelible impression.'

Of course not everyone agrees with this view, and if you have an arrangement with your friends not to write, then you are lucky indeed. On the whole it's fair to say that most hosts would feel rather peeved if their guests didn't thank them by letter. Ideally this should be handwritten and run to two sides. It will be so appreciated by your host if you really make an effort with it. Don't forget to thank for lunch too and if it was lunch at the house, organised by the host's wife, then proper form would dictate that a separate letter should be written specifically to her. If your partner or child joined you for lunch, you could always delegate that letter to them.

In conclusion

I hope this book has provided some entertainment in the form of anecdotes and quotes, to all Guns, regardless of their level of experience. I also hope that it has enabled the novice Gun to understand some of the basic as well as the lesser known aspects of this very traditional sport.

Over the past thirty years, the face of shooting has changed considerably, but the need for safety and good manners on the field is just as pertinent today as it has ever been. It's interesting to note that first and foremost on everyone's lips when I asked them what made 'the perfect guest' was safety – and good company. No one mentioned being a good shot. So you could say that all shooting etiquette boils down to safety, good sportsmanship and good manners.

This is not the first book to cover shooting etiquette, and doubtless it won't be the last, because it's a subject which is quite simply vital to the continuance of the sport. Poor sportsmanship and lack of safety on the field are the most direct routes to getting the sport banned. I feel sure that whatever happens to shooting in the future, the importance of shooting etiquette will remain just as crucial.

All that remains for me to say is: I hope you will be Asked Again… and Again!

'…*a farewell to arms.*'

Appendix

Contacts directory

Shooting organisations

British Association for Shooting and Conservation (www.basc.org.uk)

Country Land and Business Association (www.cla.org.uk)

Countryside Alliance, Campaign for Shooting (www.countryside-alliance.org.uk)

Game Farmers' Association (www.gfa.org.uk)

National Gamekeepers' Organisation (www.nationalgamekeepers.org.uk)

Scottish Gamekeepers' Association (www.scottishgamekeepers.co.uk)

The Game and Wildlife Conservation Trust (www.gct.org.uk)

Scottish Rural Property and Business Association (www.srpba.com)

Gunsmiths

AYA, Aguirre y Aranzabal	www.aya-fineguns.com
Beretta	www.beretta.com
Browning	www.browning.com
Boss Guns	www.bossguns.co.uk
E. J. Churchill	www.ejchurchillgunmakers.com
Holland and Holland	www.hollandandholland.com
Mckay Brown	www.mckaybrown.com
Purdey	www.purdey.com
Ray Ward	www.raywardgunsmith.com
Watson Bros	www.watsonbrosgunmakers.com
William and Son	www.williamandson.com
William Evans	www.williamevans.com
William Powell	www.william-powell.co.uk
Westley Richards	www.westley-richards.com

Cartridge Company, who deliver   www.caledoniancc.com

Shooting clothing and accessories

Barbour   www.barbour.com

Beretta   www.beretta.com

Cordings   www.cordings.co.uk

Dubarry   www.dubarry.com

Farlows   www.farlows.co.uk

Holland and Holland   www.hollandandholland.com

Musto   www.musto.com

Purdey   www.purdey.com

Ray Ward   www.raywardgunsmith.com

Really Wild Clothing   www.reallywildclothing.co.uk

Roxtons   www.roxtons.co.uk

Oliver Brown   www.oliverbrown.org.uk

Orvis   www.orvis.co.uk

Clay pigeon shooting grounds

Bisley Shooting Ground   www.bisleyshooting.co.uk

West London Shooting School   www.shootingschool.co.uk

E. J. Churchill   www.wwsg.org.uk

Royal Berkshire Shooting School www.rbss.co.uk

The Yorkshire Gunroom   www.yorkshiregunroom .com

Litts Treetops Shooting Ground   www.ukgunroom.com

Shooting magazines

Country Illustrated   www.countryclubuk.com

Country Life   www.countrylife.co.uk

Fieldsports   www.fieldsportsmagazine.com

Shooting Gazette   www.shootinggazette.co.uk

Sporting Gun   www.sportinggun.co.uk

Shooting Times   www.shootingtimes.co.uk

The Field   www.thefield.co.uk

Very useful shooting website   shootinguk.co.uk

Shooting agencies (for buying shooting days)

Guns on Pegs   www.gunsonpegs.com

Outside Days   www.outsidedays.com

Roxtons   www.roxtons.com

Driven Shooting   www.drivenshooting.com

Strutt and Parker   www.struttandparker.com

Author's note

By no means a definitive list, I hope that the above will be a useful starting point. Individuals will of course have their own favourite suppliers/websites.